JOINTS

A WOODWORKER'S GUIDE

RALPH LAUGHTON

GUILD OF MASTER CRAFTSMAN PUBLICATIONS LTD

In memory of Uncle Reg, a man
who loved wood

Reginald Douglas Miller 1924–1990
My uncle and my friend

First published 2018 by
Guild of Master Craftsman Publications Ltd
Castle Place, 166 High Street,
Lewes, East Sussex BN7 1XU

Previously published as *Success with Joints* (first published 2005)

ISBN 978 1 78494 441 4

Publisher: Jonathan Bailey
Production: Jim Bulley, Jo Pallet
Senior Project Editor: Virginia Brehaut
Managing Art Editor: Gilda Pacitti
Designer: Ginny Zeal

Additional photography: GMC Publications/ Anthony Bailey (cover and all full-page
photographs), John Bullar (page 5), Anthony DiChello/Shutterstock.com (page 56 top right),
Brian Goodman/Shutterstock.com (page 56 bottom right)

Colour origination by GMC Reprographics
Printed and bound in China

A note on measurements

Although care has been taken to ensure that the imperial measurements
are true and accurate, they are only conversions from metric; they have been rounded
up or down to the nearest $\frac{1}{16}$in, or to the nearest convenient equivalent in cases where the
metric measurements themselves are only approximate. When following the instructions,
use either the metric or the imperial measurements; do not mix units.

CONTENTS

Introduction

Within the pages of this book I hope to give you the knowledge and confidence you need to make the furniture and other projects that you have always wanted to build. Anybody can make beautiful joints in wood. There are no magical forces at work – just careful planning and an understanding of the mechanics of joining timber. Put that together with sharp, well-maintained tools, and you are halfway there. The other half of the equation I can't give you – that is down to you. There is no substitute for experience – good or bad, it will all teach you something.

Why learn the basics?

I was lucky enough to be schooled in the traditional processes of woodwork from the age of 11, with real tools and a teacher who loved what he was doing. The processes that we were taught, over the first couple of years, had not changed in decades, and are still as relevant today as they were then.

The main difference today is that the market is flooded with power tools intended to make woodworking easier – and so they will, providing you know how to use them properly and have a sound knowledge of the mechanical properties of the wood being used. Sadly, the use of traditional tools is being passed over in favour of more user-friendly items aimed at the vastly hyped do-it-yourself market. To compound the situation, very little formal education is given – or, for that matter, available – to the budding woodworker.

Before I had the luxury of power tools, all my woodworking was done using hand tools – that was the norm. It is wise to acquire the skill of working by hand, because that grounding will help you to get the best out of your power tools. I still often use hand tools, not for sentimental reasons but for speed and accuracy.

This book will take you through the basic techniques required to cut and fit joints by hand. Learning to cut joints properly, in the traditional manner, will allow you to evaluate the alternatives.

Timber

One of the best ways to convince yourself that cutting joints is too hard is to start with some joinery-grade softwood. (Remember: 'joinery' in this book does not mean joint-making.) This is the nondescript pine that you will find in the do-it-yourself stores and at most timber merchants. Unless your tools are super-sharp, the timber will crush and tear as you attempt to cut it.

If you want to practise your joint-making techniques, go to a specialist hardwood supplier and ask for some 'shorts' or offcuts. These will be sold at a much lower price than larger boards. Hardwood such as maple, beech and walnut will cut more easily, and give a clean finish. You will stand a much greater chance of success.

Tools

The most important tool is the **workbench**. This needs to be at a convenient height for you, and, most importantly, it must be firm. A wobbly bench will always be fighting against you, which constantly results in inferior work and costs you much more effort than would normally be required. Stability is

FOCUS ON:

British and US terminology

This book was written in London, England; you could be reading it a few streets away, or halfway around the world. In the UK, 'joinery' is the functional, decorative and sometimes structural woodwork of a building: windows, doors, architraves, panelling and so on. However, in the US 'joinery' means the art of forming joints. I am following the British usage, so none of what appears here will be referred to as 'joinery'. I also use the British term 'timber', which corresponds to the American 'lumber'.

Apart from the fact that you can never have enough of them, cramps are another one of those things that have been given a similar title in common usage. I am referring to the word 'clamp'. For me, to *cramp* is to hold something together while the glue is curing – or, in its other usage, to hold a window or door frame in position while the cement dries. To *clamp* something is to hold it still and firm.

relative to mass – a heavily constructed bench will be far more rigid than a lightweight version. Alternatively, rigidity can be borrowed from a wall or the floor by fixing the bench to either or both. The bench shown under construction here was made from softwood and MDF, and gained its amazing rigidity from being screwed to the wall.

A good **vice** is a must – without it, holding the wood firm will be almost impossible. Good-quality ones, such as the Axminster model seen in some of my photographs, perform well and are easy to fit. Holes in the right-hand leg of the bench accept a dowel to support the other end of a long board or panel held in the vice.

No matter what tools you decide to buy, always try to buy the best you can afford. One good plane is better than three mediocre models. The rule here is definitely quality, not quantity. If I were starting again today, the tools listed on the following pages are what I would buy first.

Key point

Whatever tools you buy, they cannot perform well if they are not sharp. All new edged tools, no matter what the quality, will benefit from sharpening and honing smooth to get the best possible finish on the edge. Cutting clean, crisp joints is only possible if the tools are sharp in the first place. In my previous book, *Success with Sharpening*, I explain many techniques to get, and keep, your tools performing in a manner that will enable you to cut all the joints shown in this book with ease.

ABOVE *Hardwood offcuts are ideal for practising joint cutting.*

ABOVE *This workshop-made bench gets its rigidity from the wall, to which it is firmly screwed.*

Marking and measuring

To start with, only a few basic tools will be required. Always buy the best that you can afford – it is better to have a few good tools than a toolbox full of bad ones.

In order to keep things true, a good-quality **square** is the most important tool you can own. Though often abused, this is a precision-made tool and should be treated as such. To check that the blade is perpendicular to the stock, scribe a line with the stock facing in one direction, then turn it over and scribe the same line over again. There should be no detectable deviation; if there is, reject the square.

A small engineer's square is extremely useful for marking smaller surfaces; a steel protractor and a combination set (comprising a combination square, centre-finder and protractor, all mounted on a steel rule) may have their uses, as we shall see later.

You will need a hard **pencil** – a 5H or 6H. (See page 57 for information on pencil grading.) This is a hard drafting pencil, which will hold a point and make a fine line. I also have a pencil sharpener: the old school-desk type. As a skilled craftsman, I am supposed to sharpen my pencils with a chisel (and I

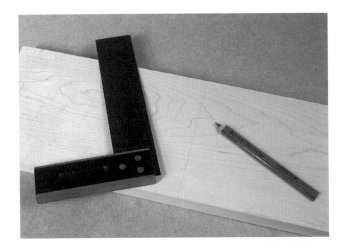

ABOVE LEFT *A small engineer's square (used here with a carpenter's pencil) is ideal for narrow surfaces.*

ABOVE RIGHT *The try square is the traditional woodworker's square. Apart from its intended use, once checked it is the benchmark for any other squares that you may use.*

RIGHT *This reasonably priced combination set offers accuracy and flexibility.*

sometimes do) but I find that the sharpener is easier. Traditional **marking knives** have a bevel on one side only, and a flat back. They are available with left- or right-hand bevels, and there are combination knives with both bevels on the same tool. I prefer the traditional type with a single bevel, and I use both left- and right-hand versions. Double bevels, such as those on utility knives, are to be avoided. The only exception to this is the use of a fine scalpel blade in those hard-to-reach places, such as when transfer-marking fine dovetail sockets (see Chapter 3:4).

BELOW *Pencil sharpeners, automatic and hand-powered.*

BELOW LEFT *Drafting pencils are good for marking, as the hard point will produce a fine line.*

BELOW RIGHT *Traditional marking knives may be bevelled on either the left or the right.*

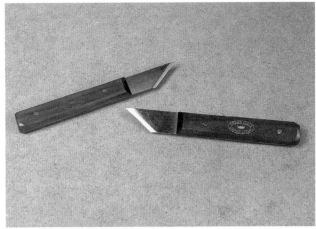

ABOVE LEFT *The screw-lock type of sliding bevel is less bulky than the lever-lock or wing-nut types, though it may not look so convenient.*

ABOVE RIGHT *Marking gauges. The rosewood and brass gauges are nice but not essential; the cheaper beech versions will do the job adequately.*

LEFT *A mortise gauge has two marking points that can be set independently. The type with the screw adjuster is easier to set than the sliding type, and is worth the extra cost.*

A **marking** and a **mortise gauge** are required as a minimum. I always recommend the use of separate gauges, as opposed to the combination gauge, which is a mortise gauge with an additional pin inserted on the opposite side of the stem so that it can also be used as a marking gauge. This practice is fine until you want to save the mortise settings for marking further mortises and tenons, but then need to use a marking gauge on something else. There is also a risk that the unused gauging point(s) will stick into your forefinger at particular settings. A cutting gauge, used for marking across the grain, is useful but not essential.

Sloping cuts are marked with the aid of a **sliding bevel**. Experience has shown that the screw-lock type of bevel, adjusted with a screwdriver, is more convenient to use than the no-tools lever-lock models, where the protruding locking mechanism can foul another surface, preventing the tool from lying flat.

Steel rules are the preferred tools for precise measuring. A 6in or 150mm rule is the most useful, as it will sit in the pocket easily and always be to hand. Longer rules are useful additions as the need arises. Retractable tape measures are not accurate enough for joint making.

FOCUS ON:
Saws

Traditional saws

A **ripsaw** has teeth sharpened to a chisel edge, filed square across the blade. It is designed to cut along (with) the grain, by chopping the fibres and carrying away the waste through the cut. A saw sharpened in this way will cut more quickly than a crosscut saw, and is less likely to stray from the intended cutting path as a result of following the grain. Saws with rip teeth are usually thought of as being large, rough-cutting saws. However, any saw that is used to cut along the grain should have its teeth sharpened to rip. A good example is the dovetail saw. Tenon saws may also be sharpened to a rip profile, for use when cutting the cheeks of a tenon, for example.

A **crosscut saw** has alternate teeth sharpened left- and right-handed to a 60° knife edge. This arrangement slices the fibres into fine pieces and dispels the waste to either side or through the saw cut. The action of a crosscut saw is less aggressive than that of a ripsaw, and it cuts more cleanly across the grain. This form is used for panel saws as well as backed saws such as tenon and 'gentlemen's' saws.

Set and kerf

To enable the saw blade to progress through the wood, the teeth are set (bent outwards) alternately to left and right, usually by one third of their thickness. This makes the cut wider than the thickness of the blade, allowing the saw easy passage through the timber without getting stuck. The cut produced by a saw is referred to as the kerf.

Hardpoint saws

Hardpoint saws are the modern alternative to the traditional saw, and although they have their place they are not ideal for fine joint making. When it comes to the heavier stuff, such as garden furniture and construction work, they are the tool to use. The 'universal' tooth pattern, although a compromise, enables them to make both rip and cross cuts. Most will also cut on the pull stroke, increasing productivity. Relatively cheap, they are regarded as throwaway items, as their very hard and brittle teeth make it impractical to resharpen and reset them once they become dull.

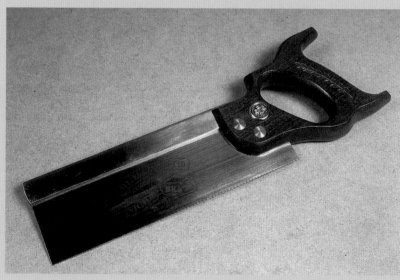

RIGHT *A tenon saw. When the teeth are ground to a crosscut configuration, it can be used for cutting the shoulders of a tenon. The saw is used for many other operations that require an accurate crosscut.*

Saws

Saws need to be sharp and have an even set. The type of saw to be used should be in proportion to the size of the joint. A small **gentleman's saw** is intended for fine cutting across the grain. At the other end of the spectrum, a large **ripsaw** is used to cut tenon cheeks, bridle joints, etc. The physical size is only half the story – what is of more importance is the tooth configuration: *crosscut* for cutting across the grain, and *rip* for cutting along the grain.

Tools which have evolved in the East are now becoming common on the shelves and in the catalogues of Western suppliers. **Japanese saws**, designed to be used from the sitting position and to cut on the pull stroke, feel a bit strange at first if, like me, you are used to the Western mode of operation. However, their rapid cutting characteristics and the fine kerf they produce are well worth the investment in time required to acquire the technique.

LEFT *A small ripsaw, sometimes called a half-rip, is the preferred tool for cutting along the grain.*

BOTTOM LEFT *Not all saws have teeth for crosscutting. This dovetail saw has very fine teeth ground for ripping along the grain.*

BOTTOM RIGHT *A rip tenon saw is a backsaw with the teeth ground to a rip profile. This saw is useful when cutting small or smallish tenons.*

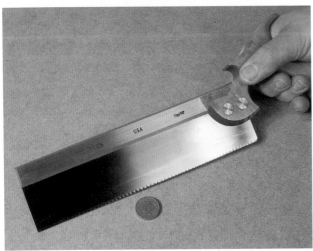

Planes

Planes are fundamental to any tool collection. Conventional **bench planes** are mostly used to prepare the timber prior to joint making – a process that is as important as cutting the joint itself. A long plane is used to flatten the surface, a shorter plane to smooth it.

There is a myriad of smaller, specialist planes available to enable access to tight places. A low-angle **block plane** with an adjustable mouth is useful for trimming end grain and for adjusting pieces to fit. One of the most useful of planes for the joint-maker is the combination rebate (rabbet), bullnose and chisel plane. This **3-in-1 plane** has been popular since its conception in the early twentieth century by Edward Preston and Sons Ltd. It was later manufactured by Record after their purchase of Preston's plane division in the 1930s. It is still in production today, made by Clico (Sheffield) Tooling Ltd and sold as a Clifton 3110.

ABOVE *Bench planes are used to dimension and finish the wood. A good starting point would be a small smoothing plane and a medium-sized jack plane. These examples are from the Clifton range of high-quality British-made tools.*

RIGHT *This Stanley low-angle block plane, with adjustable mouth, is ideal for trimming end grain.*

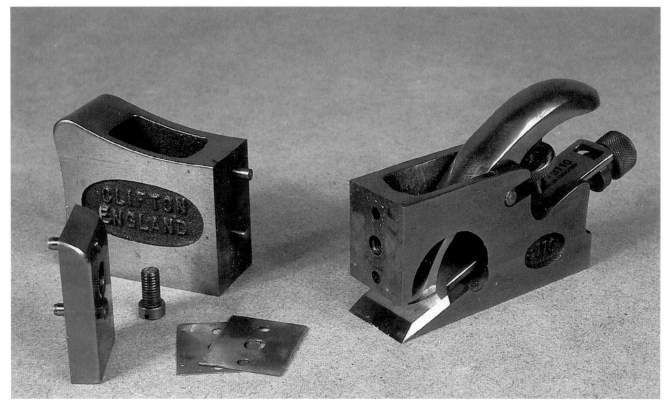

ABOVE LEFT *The Clifton 3110 combination plane in rebate/shoulder plane mode; shims are used to adjust the mouth opening.*

ABOVE RIGHT *By changing the nose the 3110 can be configured as a bullnose plane.*

ABOVE *By removing the nose altogether the 3110 becomes a very useful chisel plane.*

Many other planes are available with lots of specialist uses. You will see some of them being used within the pages of this book. However, the four planes mentioned here will cover most of what you need; other planes just make it easier.

Chisels

As with planes, there are lots of varieties to choose from. A basic set of six **bevel-edged chisels**, from 6 to 38mm ($\frac{1}{4}$ to $1\frac{1}{2}$in) wide, is always a good start; boxed sets usually show a saving compared to buying individual tools. **Mortise chisels** are best bought as

LEFT *A set of bevel-edged chisels is a good investment to start with.*

BELOW LEFT *Paring chisels are much more delicate than other chisels and are intended to be used under hand pressure only, without a mallet.*

BELOW RIGHT *Mortise chisels are of heavier construction than normal bench chisels.*

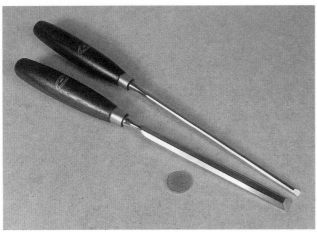

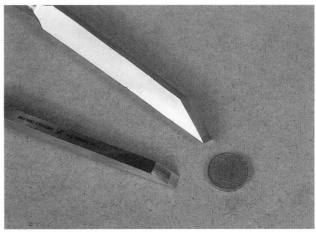

and when the need arises; they need to be the same width as the mortise you are making (see Chapter 3:3). A 10mm (³/₈in) mortise chisel is a good starting point. The more delicate **paring chisels** are useful for fine fitting, and the longer ones are excellent for flattening the bottoms of housings or dadoes (see Chapter 3:5).

The mallet

The mallet is used for persuading things to happen – not forcing them. It is used to drive a mortise chisel into the wood with a succession of light blows, not one almighty whack. Its other use is to tap two components of a joint together – which does not mean forcing a badly cut joint together. Rubber and dead-blow mallets also have their uses; the latter is a hollow, rubber-covered mallet filled with loose shot, which reduces bounce and thereby makes the blow more effective. White rubber mallets reduce the risk of marking the surface of the wood.

Cramps

Cramps are needed to apply pressure to a glued joint while it is curing. A couple of 150mm (6in) G-cramps (C-clamps in American usage) will get things going. For larger glue-ups, sash or bar cramps are required. It is a good idea to buy these in threes; this will enable you to balance the cramping pressure when using them to glue up panels.

You can never have enough cramps. Fifty years on from acquiring my first cramp, I still find I need more. Always buy the best you can afford: cheap cramps are likely to twist under load, which can distort the joint or cause it to slip. Buying your main-use cramps is definitely a case of quality outweighing quantity – though cheaper cramps can be used as a secondary means of applying pressure to a long joint.

BELOW *The raw materials for joint making: hardwood offcuts and a basic set of good-quality tools.* **Back row, left to right:** *mallet, sliding bevel, two try squares, engineer's square, cutting gauge, mortise gauge. Foreground, left to right: bevel-edged chisel, mortise chisel, combined protractor and depth gauge, marking awl, marking knife, dovetail saw, smoothing plane, 3110 combination plane, low-angle block plane.*

A basic tool kit

Setting out:
- Pencils
- Marking knife
- Try square
- Marking gauge
- Mortise gauge
- Sliding bevel
- Steel rules

Sawing:
- Ripsaw
- Tenon saw (crosscut)
- Tenon saw (rip-cut)
- Dovetail saw

Planing:
- Jack plane
- Smoothing plane
- Block plane
- 3-in-1 plane

Chopping and paring:
- Bevel-edged chisels
- Mortise chisels
- Paring chisels
- Beech mallet

Cramping:
- 2 G-cramps
- 3 sash cramps

Before you start

There are some tools that you can make for yourself: the bench hook, the mitre block and various types of shooting boards.

Bench hook

The bench hook has a number of uses:

· It is used to hold timber for sawing.
· The flat area is used for chopping or drilling into, to protect the bench top.
· If you make it accurately enough, it can be used as an **end shoot** for squaring the end of a length of timber, using the side of the bench hook as a guide for the plane.

Over the years you will construct lots of bench hooks of various sizes. They are probably the most versatile tool you can build using just three pieces of wood. Make a simple one from planed softwood, with stops screwed and glued to it, square to the edge. One stop runs the full width of the board; this enables it to be used as an end shoot. The other is cut short to allow wood to be sawn to length without cutting into the bench. You will see this simple bench hook, and variations on it, being used throughout this book.

Mitre block

A mitre block is used for cutting stock of small cross section at a predetermined angle, usually 45°. The angle can be varied to suit the job in hand: for example, it can be increased to 60° for making a hexagonal frame or 67.5° for an octagonal one. Dimensions will vary according to use, but most mitre blocks are small enough to be used in conjunction with a bench hook.

The traditional method of making a mitre block is to rebate (rabbet) a block of hardwood and cut the mitre guides into the resultant upstand. Your local hardwood supplier may have offcuts which will do the job, at a fraction of the price of longer boards. Careful marking and sawing of the guide slots is important. Cutting the slots before the block is rebated will allow for easier marking out, and the greater width will minimize any error.

The reason for making the block from one solid piece is one of stability; but with today's materials it is easier to make the mitre block from two pieces. MDF or cabinet-grade plywood can be used for the base, while a hardwood offcut for the fence, with the mitre slots cut into it, can be screwed and glued in place. A loose strip of sheet material is placed in the rebate to raise the workpiece to the bottom of the slots. This can then be discarded and replaced with a fresh piece whenever it becomes tatty through repeated use.

Shooting boards

The purpose of a shooting board or 'shoot' is to support timber at a predetermined angle in order that it can be planed. It is used when the surface area to be planed is too small to bear the sole of the plane adequately. In its simplest form it is used to square the edges of thin stock. The addition of stops and fences will enable it to be used to fine-tune angled cuts which have been made using the mitre block.

The simplest form of shoot can be made from two pieces of MDF screwed together to form a rebate large enough to hold your chosen plane lying on its side. The upper piece should have a hardwood edging strip applied to reduce wear. Again the size of the shoot will vary according to what it is to be used for. Several variations will be seen throughout the book, and their construction will be detailed as necessary.

1
Planning
& Preparation

1:1
Planning the work

1:2
Preparing the wood

1:1
Planning the work

The first joint I ever made was done with a hammer and nails. The hammer was a rather short-handled club hammer and the nails were recovered from a bucket under the bench. After nailing the two pieces of wood, which had fallen off the garden gate, together, I was off to battle with my new sword. I was about to discover two things: nails are not intended to hold the hilt onto a newly crafted sword, and grown-ups don't have the same perspective on life as a six-year-old!

Some years later, after the emotions of that day had diminished into a family tale that comes out each Christmas ('Do you remember the day…'), my uncle – owner of the gate – showed me how to join those two pieces of wood together without any nails. By this time I must have been eight and a quarter. He used a simple halved joint, tight enough that it did not need any glue to hold it together – though the strength of the joint was further improved with the application of glue.

I had discovered the art of joint making. More important, although not so obvious at the time, was the lesson in how to apply jointing methods: the two pieces of wood could have been joined in several ways, but the halving joint gave the strength required with a minimum of effort.

Economy of labour

The halving joint used to make my sword was all that was required for the purpose. Fancy joint cutting would not have improved the strength of the joint, but would just have taken longer to execute. In this situation the joint is under a minimum of stress and is purely cosmetic in function – it just holds the crosspiece in position to represent the hilt.

In other situations, no mechanical strength is built into the joint at all – the surfaces are simply squared up and glued together. This form of joining is only successful when the grain of the pieces to be joined is parallel at the point at which they make contact. A solid table top can be assembled in this way. The edges of the boards are planed as near to flat and square as possible (this is called edge-jointing). Glue is applied and the boards are cramped together. If conducted in a careful manner, with an appropriate type of glue, this joint can be as strong as the board itself, and in many cases stronger.

Tonguing and grooving this type of joint will not improve its strength. In fact, unless all the mating surfaces are in perfect contact with each other, it

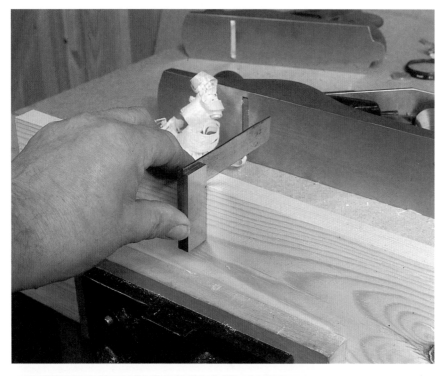

LEFT *Joining boards side by side using glue only.*

BELOW LEFT *Boards are squared ready for gluing and cramping.*

BELOW RIGHT *The joint is checked to see that there are no voids. Performed correctly, this most basic form of joint is very strong.*

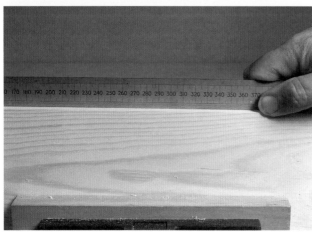

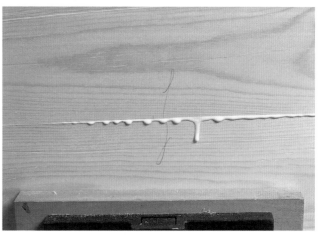

may even weaken it. Loose tongues, biscuits or dowels will not add strength either, but can be used to aid alignment; when using stock that is slightly warped or twisted, this can save a lot of cleaning up later.

The further away from parallel the grain of the gluing surfaces is, the weaker the joint will be. A 45° mitre will be significantly weaker than an edge joint. An end-grain glue joint has virtually no strength at all. It is at this point that the timber needs to be fashioned to make the assembly stronger – by cutting a joint.

BELOW LEFT *Long-grain joints – where the grain of both components is parallel to the gluing surface – are the strongest.*

BELOW RIGHT *As the joint surface moves away from being parallel to the grain, the glue joint becomes weaker. At 45° – a conventional mitre joint – the strength is highly compromised.*

BOTTOM *An end-grain glue joint has virtually no strength whatsoever.*

When building functional items, appearance is not the prime concern. Obviously the finished thing ought to look neat and well-built, but the function is the prime concern. A workbench is a good example of this. The fact that the joints are visible is not so important – the emphasis is on strength and rigidity.

When building furniture, the rules are slightly different. Strength is still important, but so is appearance. A four-legged table is similar in principle to the workbench. Here, however, visual considerations are far more important, and careful thought must be given to the type of joints that are employed and how they will look.

BELOW *Mortise and tenon joinery is used here to join the legs to the rails of a small hall table, achieving both strength and elegance.*

A joint for every purpose

In order to decide what sort of joint to employ in any given instance, the expected use needs to be taken into consideration. Does it need to be super-strong under all conditions, or just in one particular situation?

Joining pieces of timber at right angles to make a frame is one of the basic techniques employed by the woodworker. If the timber is merely **butted and glued** together, with the end grain making one of the mating surfaces, the joint will be weak, having very little shear strength and even less tensional resistance. Halving the thickness of each piece will allow them to be lapped over each other, providing a much larger gluing area and creating a stronger joint. This **halving or lap joint** is the simplest of joints, and has many uses where strength and aesthetics are of only moderate importance.

ABOVE *A cross-grain (end grain to long grain) butt joint will have very little strength.*

ABOVE *Halving the joint will improve the strength by providing more gluing surface and a degree of mechanical support.*

ABOVE *A bridle joint will further improve the joint by supplying mechanical strength from opposing sides.*

FOCUS ON:
Why joints fail

Apart from glue failure, joints usually fail due to bad design, either using the wrong joint or in the wrong orientation. A joint in **compression** (being pressed together by outside forces) is unlikely to fail. The material's strength is the governing factor. If the joint is in **tension** (being pulled apart) then the design of the joint as well as the material strength need to be considered.

By far the most testing time for a joint is when it is subjected to **shear** – a sideways or twisting force. In this situation, material strength as well as good joint design are important.

Most joints are subjected to a combination of all three forces. A joint will fail if it is subject to excessive force outside its original design, or if proper consideration is not paid to the stresses placed on it in the first place.

BELOW LEFT *A dovetailed lap joint will give the same support as the halving joint, but with the addition of tensional strength.*

BELOW RIGHT *Sliding dovetail joints provide plenty of tensional strength and form a strong support if cut well.*

BOTTOM *Face frames for cabinets require strength and also need to be aesthetically pleasing. Blind mortise and tenon joints will achieve both aims.*

Where more strength is required, a still larger glue surface can be obtained by using a **bridle joint**. This joint divides the thickness of the timber into three by means of a slot in one piece and a tongue in the other, thus doubling the glue area in comparison with a halved joint and providing mechanical support from two opposed directions.

If tensional strength is the requirement – that is, if you need to prevent one component being pulled out of the other – a **dovetail joint** is more appropriate. This can be in the form of a dovetailed halving joint, providing mechanical strength in two

adjacent directions, or a sliding through dovetail; both provide mechanical strength in tension. More sophisticated frames employ **mortise and tenon joints**, making a strong frame with joints that are invisible, in the case of blind mortises.

All the joints discussed so far use glue to complete the bond. In some cases – as when making a joint which needs to be disassembled from time to time – it is not practical to glue the joint. In such situations, wedges and keys are used to expand or lock the joint. Country-style tables and benches employ **tusk tenons** and **wedged tenons** to hold the components together.

BELOW *No-glue joints. In this oak stool the stretchers are secured to the legs with tusk tenons. A wedge-shaped key is driven through a square hole in the protruding tenon to tighten the joint.*

BOTTOM *Wedges are used to expand the tenons which secure the legs to the top of the oak stool.*

BELOW LEFT *A mitred joint on the corner of a large box has little strength.*

BELOW RIGHT *Adding a loose tongue or spline to a mitred panel joint will aid alignment, but add little to the strength considering the amount of work involved.*

BOTTOM *Secret dovetails would add a great deal of strength, but the amount of work needed would be vast – this type of joint is best used for smaller projects such as jewellery boxes.*

Joining panels together requires a range of techniques. To take an everyday example, a toy box with a hinged lid will need to be strong and child-friendly. The timber used to make the sides, ends, lid and bottom can be edge-glued to make up panels of the required width. Joining these panels together to make the box can be achieved in several ways. A mitred corner would make an invisible joint, but would be lacking in strength without extra support. This could be supplied by inserting a loose tongue or spline, but the work involved would outweigh the

minimal increase in strength. Secret dovetails would improve the strength greatly, but are time-consuming and unnecessary. Conventional through dovetails would also work, but the easiest and most practical method would be to use **finger joints**. Their regular appearance from each side makes for a neat, symmetrical look, and provides plenty of glue area, resulting in a strong, practical joint appropriate to the purpose of the box. The most important of the joints mentioned above are described in detail in Part 3.

BELOW *Through dovetails are a viable option...*

BOTTOM LEFT *...but the finger joint must be the favourite for ease of cutting and resultant strength.*

BOTTOM RIGHT *Cutting a stack of finger joints will speed up production.*

Working efficiently

Try to get a production line going whenever you can. If you have 20 similar mortises and tenons to cut, do all the mortises first, then change your tools and cut all the tenons. This method of batch production will speed the joint-cutting process considerably. Materials for other joints can be stacked on the bench and cut one after the other in a single session. The finger joints used in the construction of the toy box can be cut using this method: stack the pieces to cut the first half of each corner, then use the resultant pieces to mark out the opposing cut.

Cutting a joint is one thing; putting it together is another. Make sure that you have enough time to assemble the joints before your chosen adhesive has started to cure. This period is called the 'open time' of the adhesive, and is usually stated on the label or in any accompanying literature. Complicated, time-consuming glue-ups are usually tackled in stages, making up components into subassemblies first; the subassemblies are then glued together to complete the construction. As well as allowing for the limitations of the glue, this practice is also economical with cramps.

BELOW *Split complicated glue-ups into subassemblies. This will not only give you more time to check the assembly, but will also save on cramps – and who has ever had enough cramps?*

Order of work

The individual joint is only part of the story: most of the time, one joint is worked in conjunction with another, and a whole mass of joints all contribute to the form and structure of the finished item. When building anything, the order in which the work is undertaken must be considered at the outset – otherwise the integrity of form and, more importantly, structural strength can be severely compromised. As far as joints are concerned, there are two factors worthy of consideration:

· the order in which the joint itself is cut
· the order in which the component parts
  of the joint are assembled.

Cutting the joint

The order in which the components of a joint are cut depends on which part is easier or more practical to trim in order to get a good fit. With simple joints this is not an issue: a notched or halving joint, for example, has two identical parts. In such cases it is best practice to cut both components on the tight side and trim them to fit each other.

Moving up the scale of complexity slightly, a bridle joint has components that are cut as opposites: what is removed from one piece must be filled by the other. In this case the open mortise is cut first and finished to the chosen size. The tongue is then cut slightly oversize and carefully trimmed until the desired fit is obtained. The same logic can be applied to mortise and tenon joints and other similar arrangements: the job is much easier to control if all the areas that need to be trimmed are on the *outside* faces. Trimming the inside of a mortise to fit the tenon is much harder because access is restricted.

BELOW LEFT *It is easier to shave the tenon to fit the mortise than it is to open up the mortise to fit the tenon.*

BELOW RIGHT *A simple housing joint or a notched joint has only one cut component, which is intended to accept the entire thickness of another piece of timber. In this case there is no option but to enlarge the housing carefully until the required fit is achieved.*

FOCUS ON:
Open time

A further complication is the time it takes to apply the glue to the joints and set them ready for cramping, compared with the open time of the glue (that is, the length of time the glue remains workable after application). This can vary from a few seconds to many hours. Most woodworkers are familiar with the white or yellow polyvinyl acetate (PVA) glues. These are formulated with differing open times, and are usually marketed with this feature as one of their selling points. A typical open time is usually stated on the container, but temperature and humidity can and do greatly affect these stated times. The characteristics of the various glues are covered in greater depth in Chapter 2:3.

If there is a risk that the overall assembly time will exceed the adhesive's open time, then break the job down into subassemblies. If this is not possible, you must either change the order of work so that the job can be divided into subassemblies, or find an alternative glue with a longer open time.

The same principle can be applied to most joints as a first consideration. However, there are occasions where this is not practical. A good example is a housing joint (a dado joint in American usage), where the entire thickness of one board is sunk into a transverse groove in another piece of timber. Since the board has already been thicknessed to the required dimension, the housing must be trimmed until the board is a good fit.

Assembly

The order in which the components are assembled needs to be considered at the same time as the choice of joint. Opposing joints will put strain on one another during glue-up if the assembly has to be twisted to locate badly positioned or awkwardly orientated joints. Sometimes an open mortise, which can be assembled from many directions, may work better than a common mortise, which can only be engaged correctly from one direction.

ABOVE *A dry run of the whole assembly will highlight any errors prior to the glue-up.*

The dry run

During the making and fitting processes, assembling each joint as an individual unit will, of course, prove that the joint works and show up any anomalies. These anomalies can be anything from uneven shoulders preventing the joint from seating properly to more serious errors in size or position. All of this can be dealt with as you continue through the build.

This dry fitting is good practice but will not show up any minor errors of alignment. Assume, for example, that a halving joint is being cut at 67.5° on each end of a piece of timber, as part of an eight-section glue-up to form an octagonal frame. If the joints are cut at 68° (just 0.5° of error), this discrepancy will be invisible to the eye, and each joint will appear to dry-fit perfectly. It will not become evident that there is anything wrong until the octagon is being glued and cramped. A complete dry run prior to gluing will show up the error in good time, before the components are covered in glue.

Making a dry run will also help you to estimate the build time and show up any potential problems in the order of assembly.

Cramping should also be planned at this stage. It is a good idea to cramp the whole assembly as if it were being glued; this will give you the chance to rearrange things as necessary without having to worry about the glue going off. This will enable you to arrive at the best possible arrangement, and have all the cramps at hand and set to the correct opening for speedy fitting and cramping once the glue has been applied.

BELOW *The cramps used to test the dry glue-up are now all to hand and set ready for work. This will speed the glue-up and enable more to be achieved during the open time of the adhesive.*

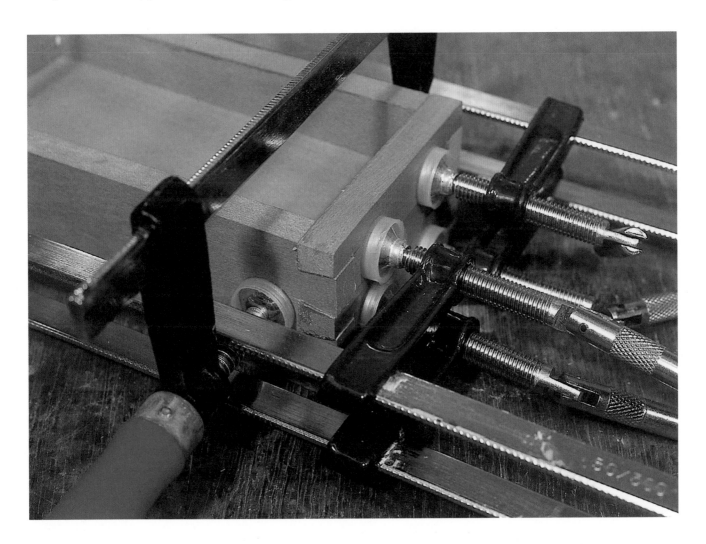

1:2
Preparing the wood

Clean, crisp joint making is the result of many factors. Accurate marking and sharp tools have already been mentioned. Just as importantly, the timber itself must be carefully prepared.

Hardwoods are usually sold as sawn boards. Most suppliers will prepare stock at additional cost, but hand planing will still be needed to achieve a silky-smooth finish – the rotary action of the planing machine will have left the surface slightly rippled.

Softwood is usually purchased planed all round, meaning that it has been machine-prepared from sawn stock. This process will often leave slight rippling and machining marks, as with hardwood. The size may also vary from piece to piece, and even from end to end of the same piece. Softwood from a timber merchant or builder's yard is usually of joinery grade, not furniture grade. Generally speaking, more knots, waney edges and checks are considered acceptable in joinery-grade timber, and the moisture content is likely to be higher. Furniture-grade softwood needs to be purchased from specialist suppliers, and is sold as sawn boards. Good-quality softwood is not a cheap option – quality timber commands a higher price, regardless of species.

Using joinery-grade timber to make furniture is not to be ruled out completely. I have used it for all sorts of projects, selecting the best-looking timber and rejecting the rest. It needs to be acclimatized to the conditions in which it will be used; this may take some time if the timber has a high moisture content.

ABOVE *Most PAR softwood is used in the building industry, and is not of the quality required for furniture making – though further drying and preparation may make it suitable.*

ABOVE *The rippled surface of a machined board may be more or less pronounced, depending on the species and the method of planing employed.*

ABOVE *Poor-quality timber may have numerous knots and checks, and is usually prone to warping and twisting as well.*

RIGHT *Joinery-grade timber can be used to make furniture, providing the pieces are carefully selected and allowances are made for the expected movement.*

Preparing the components

Once the timber has been acclimatized to the conditions in which it will be used, the components for your project can be prepared. Select some suitable boards from your stock and mark out the components. Try to make the most economical use of each board, but always allow some extra material in case of mistakes. Rough-trim the various parts from the stock boards and label them if necessary; you may find it helpful to use the triangle method described on page 64.

FOCUS ON:

Moisture content

Movement – warping and shrinkage of timber – is caused by the wood absorbing or releasing moisture from, or into, its surroundings. Wood will absorb moisture if its surroundings have a higher moisture content than itself; this will cause it to expand. The converse is also true: if the wood has a higher moisture content than its surroundings, it will release moisture and shrink. This movement is most significant across the grain; lengthwise, the movement is for the most part insignificant. If the wood is allowed to acclimatize to its environment over a period of time, it will become stable, no longer releasing or absorbing moisture – as long as the environment remains stable. At this stage the wood is said be at equilibrium moisture content (EMC).

Wood should be dried so as to match, as near as possible, the surroundings in which the finished product is going to be used. By doing this the subsequent period of acclimatization will be shortened. There are no hard-and-fast rules here, as the moisture content will vary greatly depending where in the world you are working. In the UK, for example, in a heated domestic environment, a moisture content of around 12% would be a good start.

In an ideal world we would store and use all our wood in a stable environment. This is not possible in the real world – but if we start with the raw materials as near to EMC as possible, the variation due to seasonal or local changes will be minimized.

RIGHT *Always check the moisture content near the centre of the board – the ends will be dryer, as moisture is released and absorbed more quickly through end grain.*

Establishing a face side and edge

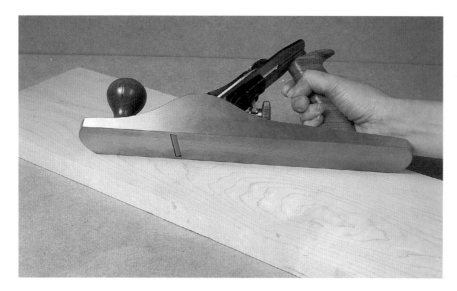

1 Select a component, inspect it carefully and choose the better side, paying attention to grain and figure matching. This is referred to as the face side. Check that the surface is flat using a steel rule or the arris of a long plane, and correct by planing if necessary.

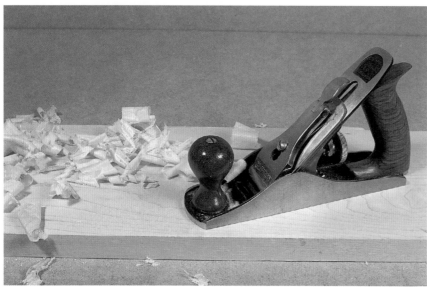

2 Using a finely set plane, smooth the surface to remove any machining marks.

3 Once the surface is flat and smooth, it is marked as the face side. The mark used varies slightly in form, depending on who has inscribed it – rather like a signature – but in essence it is a stylized lower-case *f*.

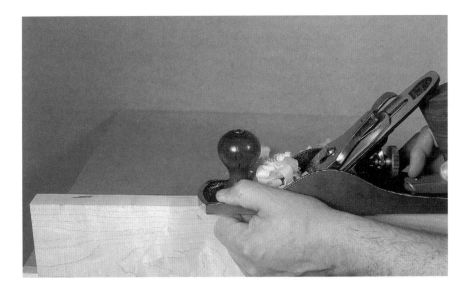

4 The tail of the face mark runs off the face, pointing to the chosen face edge. The face edge is planed straight ('shot'), using a long plane, ensuring that the edge is kept square to the face side.

5 Always place the stock of the try square on the face side and check the edge with the blade at various points along its length.

6 Once the edge has been planed square to the face side, it is marked as the face edge with an inverted V. The V should point towards the face side mark, and all subsequent marking should be referenced from one of these two faces.

Dimensioning the timber

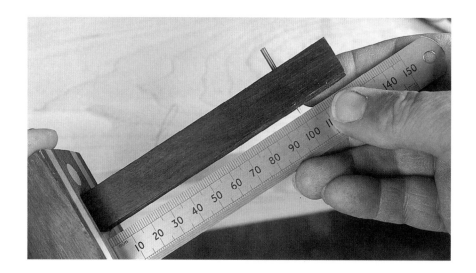

1 To mark the width, set a marking gauge to the required dimension using a steel rule. *Lightly* tighten the securing screw of the gauge and recheck the setting. Minor adjustments can be made by holding the stock (head) of the gauge and gently tapping the stem on the bench. Once the gauge is correctly set, fully tighten the locking screw.

TECHNIQUE:
Squaring an edge

As a guide when squaring the edge, scribe pencil lines across the timber before making a cut. The marks will be removed only from the areas where the plane is cutting. By tipping the plane very slightly, the angle of cut can be corrected until the edge is square to the face side. When planing timber that is narrower than the sole of the plane, it is advisable to hold the plane between the thumb and forefinger alongside the front knob; this will make it easier to control the angle of attack. If the timber is very thin, a shooting board is used to support the plane and the workpiece. (This is similar to the mitre shooting board on page 112, but with a square rather than an angled stop.) Shooting the edge may take a bit of time to get right if this is your first attempt, but don't give up.

ABOVE *By first scribing lines across the edge with a pencil, it is possible to see exactly where material is being removed by the plane.*

2 Use the gauge to scribe the wood to the correct width. This is done by registering the stock on the face edge and lightly scribing the timber by sliding the gauge along the length of the piece. Keep the stock tight against the face edge, as the point is likely to try and follow the grain of the timber. Rotate the stem of the gauge so that the point trails and does not dig in too deeply.

3 Saw off the waste just outside the gauged line.

4 The piece is finished down to the line with a plane. The new edge is checked for square and straightness throughout this final planing process.

5 With one face and two edges planed and square to each other, your piece of timber can now be thicknessed. Registering the stock of the marking gauge against the face side, mark the thickness on both edges. Either use a second marking gauge for this, or make sure you have marked all the pieces to width before changing the setting to mark the thickness. Marking the end also may help on wider boards, but is theoretically unnecessary, as constant checking with the try square should keep the face flat.

6 If there is a lot of material to take away, use a saw to remove the bulk of the waste to just outside the scribed line.

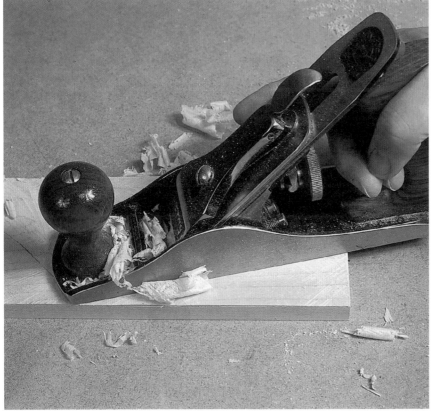

7 Then use planes to flatten and smooth the surface and finish to the line. Keep checking your progress with a straightedge and a try square at every stage of the planing process.

Squaring the ends

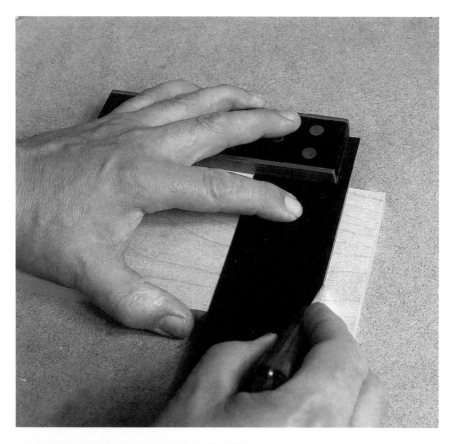

1 With a try square and marking knife, cut a line across the face side with the stock of the square registered on the face edge. Then cut a line down the face edge with the stock of the square registered on the face side. To ensure that the second cut is exactly aligned with the first, a useful trick is to place the knife in the existing cut and slide the square up to it. Continue the marks all the way round the piece, ensuring that the stock of the try square is always registering on the face side or edge. Assuming the timber has been perfectly prepared, the lines will meet up all the way around. Mark the waste side of the line with pencil hatching.

2 Place the timber on the bench hook and, using a tenon saw, carefully square the end. As always, cut on the waste side of the line. The knife-cut line not only indicates the position of the cut, but also severs the grain of the timber, preventing the saw teeth from breaking out the fibres of the wood and creating a rough edge.

3 The end grain can now be planed smooth. Care needs to be exercised here to prevent the plane from chipping off the unsupported end of the timber as it passes over. To avoid this, either plane into the centre from each side so that the plane does not pass over the end, or clamp a piece of scrap to the end so that the end fibres are supported as the plane passes over them. You can pare the end with a chisel if it is too small to plane easily.

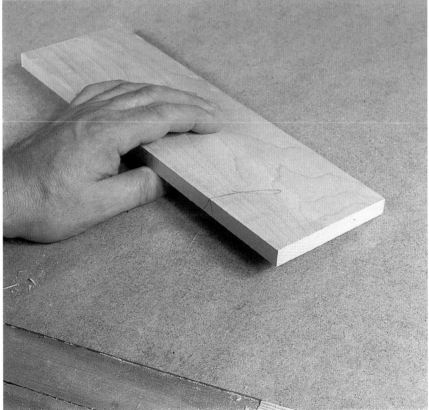

4 You should now have a perfectly square piece of timber ready to be used.

2

Basic Techniques
of Joint Making

2:1
Measurement & marking

2:2
Cutting & fitting

2:3
Glues, cramps & assembly

2:1
Measurement & marking

There is no such thing as 'nearly right': something is either right or, if it is not right, it is wrong. However, when measuring anything, a certain amount of tolerance is acceptable, and in most cases necessary. An engineer machining steel may be aiming to be accurate within a specified number of thousandths of an inch, say plus or minus two 'thou' (± 0.002in, or 0.05mm). This leeway is known as a 'machining tolerance', and allows for discrepancies in the machining and for external factors such as expansion and contraction of the material. The machining is deemed to be 'right' if it is within those tolerances.

A similar ethic must be applied to working with wood. For hand work the tolerances usually need to be a bit wider than a few thousandths of an inch, but the principle is the same. The woodworker must *aim* to be spot-on, but an acceptable tolerance must be applied. Just what that tolerance is will depend on the job, the type of material and the finish required. Four thousandths of an inch (0.004in or 0.1mm) is just about as fine as you could expect to achieve; 10 thou or one hundredth of an inch (0.01in or 0.25mm) is a more realistic starting point.

I am sure some people will claim that even tighter tolerances are possible, but of course the ultimate aim is perfection – any tolerances are only realistic guidelines that should be used as a basis for constant improvement.

Marking the wood

In the normal course of events, the woodworker first gets to grips with the material at the point where the timber has been felled, converted into boards and at least partly seasoned. The first thing to do is to inspect the boards and mark any defects such as checks, splits, dead knots, wormholes and the like. This is best done with chalk or a crayon. Then it is out with the tape measure, soft pencil and large square to mark up the wood for rough cutting and subsequent preparation. The marking is not going to be very accurate at this stage, as the board is not finished, so an allowance for waste must be built into each dimension.

When working on certain projects – such as garden furniture and other outdoor items – it is sometimes necessary to use and mark green (unseasoned) wood. This can be tricky with a conventional pencil. Although a soft pencil will do the job, it is usually easier to make the marks with a joiner's awl and a marking knife.

It is after this preparatory stage that the measuring and marking processes take on a whole new level of accuracy. From here on the tape measure is banned, and only good-quality steel rules are up to the standard required. An engineer's square and protractor will also come in useful.

BELOW *Coarse to fine measuring: timber is measured with a tape measure, callipers, rules and many other devices.*

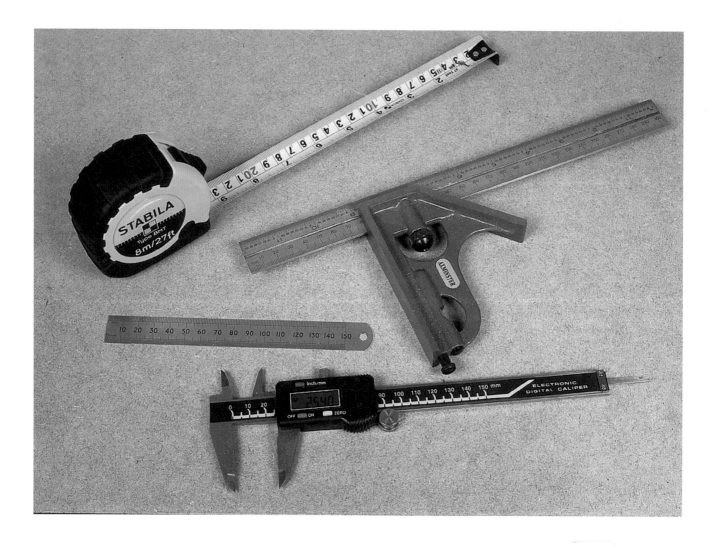

BELOW *Inspecting and marking a sawn board for defects prior to selecting the most economical cutting plan.*

RIGHT *Marking green timber with a joiner's awl and a marking knife.*

BOTTOM *Using a good-quality steel rule, try squares, engineer's square and protractor is the best way to ensure accuracy of measurement and marking.*

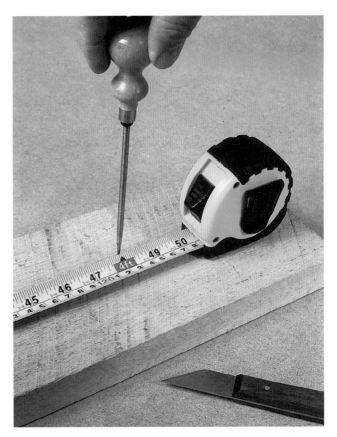

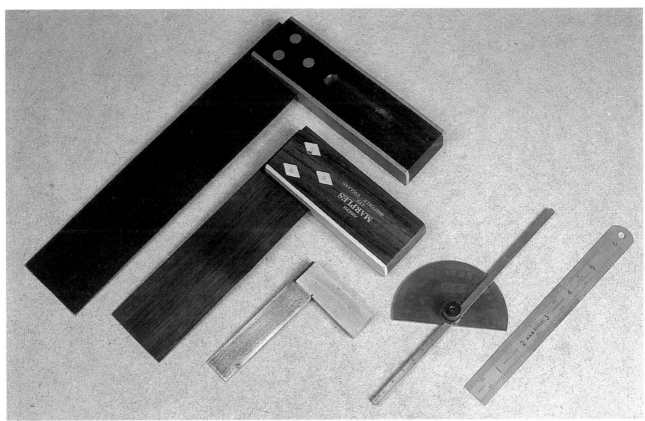

Tools for marking

Pencils, knives and points

The carpenter's traditional rectangular-section pencil is also set aside at this stage. If a pencil is used at all for the marking of joints, a good hard grade (4H or above) is required. This is used to make light markings which are then 'confirmed' with a marking knife prior to cutting. Wherever possible, it is better to use a marking knife or a sharp, slender awl instead of a pencil. A softer pencil is useful for making face and edge marks and for general referencing of the order of assembly.

Sharpening pencils with a utility knife or a chisel is also the site carpenter's domain. A decent pencil sharpener will give a good strong point every time, quickly and easily. When special attention to the pencil point is required, the scalpel is the tool of preference. The scalpel is also used for transferring marks from one component of a joint to the yet uncut receiving piece. This is particularly useful when using the tails of a fine dovetail joint to mark the position of the pins (see Chapter 3:4).

FOCUS ON:
Parallax error

If two points are viewed from differing angles their relative proximity to each other will appear to change; this is called 'parallax'. This can lead to error when marking distances from a steel rule, unless the eyeline is absolutely perpendicular to the face of the rule. The more extreme the angle of vision, the greater the error; at 45° the error will be equal to the thickness of the rule. For this reason it is better to sight the marks from in front of the rule where possible. Using the thinner 6in (150mm) rule will also minimize the parallax effect.

ABOVE *A thin rule, like the one on the left, will reduce the parallax effect.*

ABOVE *Soft pencils (B grades) are useful for marking waste and other indications.*

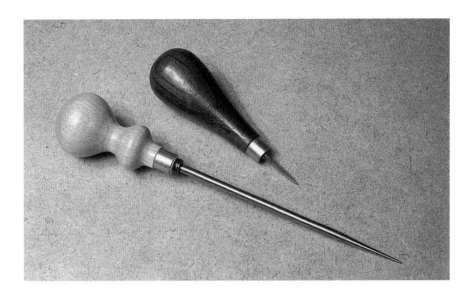

LEFT *A slender awl is a good marking tool, as it will retain its point – but do not put it in your pocket!*

Pencil grading

In Europe, pencils are graded in H and B numbers. English pencil makers started to use letters to grade pencils in degrees of hardness in the early 1800s: soft pencils were classified B (black), and harder pencils H (hard). The harder the lead, the more Hs it had (e.g. HHHH); the softer the lead, the more Bs it had. I assume that counting the Hs on a very hard pencil, or the Bs on a very soft one, became tiresome, so by the beginning of the 1900s the familiar two-digit system was introduced: HHHH became 4H, and so on.

The modern European grades start in the middle with HB and progress up the scale, getting harder, as H, 2H, 3H, etc. up to 9H. Going the other way we have B, 2B, 3B, etc. up to 9B. Just to confuse the issue, there is an odd grade F that sits between H and HB and is used as a slightly harder HB for when notation or writing is involved.

The American grading is done using numbers only. As a guide, the US #2 is roughly equivalent to the European HB; higher numbers are harder. There is not a hard and fast standard for these grades, and as a result the consistency from one manufacturer to another can vary.

Carpenters' pencils are commonly sold in three grades, colour-coded and/or marked accordingly: soft (blue), medium (red) and hard (green). The soft, being deep into the B grades, is used for marking green wood or sawn timber. The medium is around the HB grade and is for general use on softwoods. The hard is up in the high Hs and is used for marking hardwoods; it is also useful on abrasive surfaces such as plaster or masonry.

Although I use carpenters' pencils from time to time, for fine work I prefer a sharp 6H drafting pencil, followed by a marking knife.

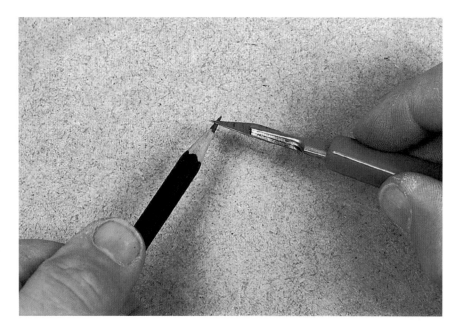

LEFT *A scalpel is used for refining the point on a pencil for special jobs...*

LEFT *...or as a marking knife when access is restricted.*

FOCUS ON:
Marking from a true face

Once the timber has been properly prepared (see Chapter 1:2), the face side and edge should be flat and true as well as being perfectly square to each other. The purpose of the face marks is to identify these two surfaces which have been used as a reference when gauging the other sides. In an ideal world the other faces would be just as square as the first two; however, any small difference (tolerance) is likely to be compounded if these other faces are used as reference surfaces in subsequent operations. For this reason **all marking should be referenced from the previously marked face side or face edge**. In practice this means registering the stock of the square or gauge on these faces and marking from there.

1 *All sides of the prepared timber should be marked from the face side and edge. Mark the face side from the face edge...*

2 *...the face edge from the face side...*

3 *...the far edge from the face side...*

4 *...and the bottom from the face edge.*

RIGHT *Using the sliding bevel to capture an angle from an existing piece of furniture.*

BELOW *The captured angle can now be transferred to the job in hand.*

Sliding bevel

The sliding bevel can be used to transfer an angle from an existing joint or finished piece to the workpiece, without measurement. It can also be set to a predetermined ratio or angle. When used to transfer angles from existing pieces, the bevel is unlocked, positioned against the surfaces to be copied, and simply locked back into position; the angle can now be marked on the new workpiece.

Transferring angles in this manner can be useful if a part needs to be fitted to a static feature such as a door surround or a piece of built-in furniture.

Marking a piece of board with a desired slope, set out as a ratio, will provide a master template to which the sliding bevel can be set when needed. This is particularly useful when marking the tails of a dovetail joint, which are usually expressed as a ratio, such as 1 : 6 or 1 : 8.

When an unusual angle needs to be marked, the sliding bevel can be set using a protractor. Alternatively, if you are familiar with trigonometry, you can use it to construct the required angle on a piece of sheet material which is then used as a setting board.

LEFT *Setting the sliding bevel to a ratio determined by a setting board.*

BELOW *When the required angle is known, the sliding bevel can be set using a protractor; the one on this combination set is particularly handy.*

Waste management

After spending time and effort preparing a piece of wood for joint making and then carefully marking and confirming the cut lines with a knife, it is good practice to mark all the waste areas by hatching with a pencil. It is very easy to cut on the wrong side of the line if the piece has been turned around a few times. The amount of time and frustration you will save over the years by marking waste areas will be enormous.

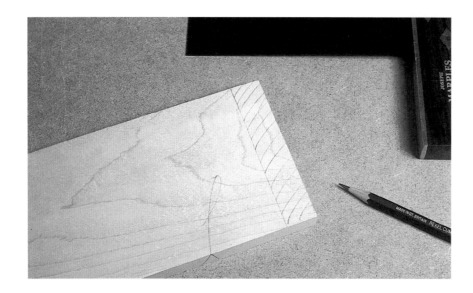

LEFT *Confirm the pencil line with a marking knife.*

The cut line

Confirming the line with a knife severs the wood fibres at the surface, leaving a clean cut across the grain. Any saw cuts should be made on the waste side of the line and slightly shy of it, leaving material to be shaved away with a chisel or plane at the fitting stage. It is best to stop short when sawing to a line, as on the tongue and shoulder of a tenon; again, final trimming is accomplished with an edged tool.

LEFT *Getting into the habit of marking all waste areas will save you the anguish of cutting to the wrong side of the line.*

Assembly marks

As the joints are cut and fitted to each other, some kind of marking system must be employed to ensure that the joints are assembled with their matching components. It does not matter what symbols are used, so long as it is clear which way round they are to be read; if using numbers, always underline 6 and

9 to denote their intended orientation. The components can be marked A–A, 1–1 or whatever you like, so long as the parts come together in the correct order and each matches the partner to which it has been fitted.

LEFT *Always cut on the waste side of the line and on the outside of the cut.*

LEFT *Square the cut to the line with a chisel or plane.*

Witness marks are applied to the job after the fitting and matching of an assembly or subassembly. On adjoining components, a simple strike across the joint with a pencil prior to dismantling will show their intended orientation and position relative to each other when they are reassembled.

If more than two components of similar dimensions are to be joined, then the marking system needs to be upgraded so as to indicate the position of each component in sequence. An example of this would be a table top made up from several consecutive boards: here the witness marks can be multiplied to accommodate the extra joints by doubling and trebling the strikes across the joints of subsequent boards.

With several boards to join, this method can become a bit tedious and lead to mistakes. A better method is to draw a triangle across the boards. The bottom of the triangle is drawn on the first board and the sides are extended across the intermediate boards so that the tip of the triangle indicates the final board.

Other forms of witness marking can be used to indicate frame or trim positions. For example, an octagonal picture frame could have its components marked 1–8 in a clockwise direction. There are no hard and fast rules here – common sense is the key to success.

LEFT *Joints must be marked to identify their matched parts.*

LEFT *Witness marks struck across the joints of adjacent boards will ensure that the correct assembly order is maintained.*

LEFT *For multiple assemblies a triangle drawn over all the pieces is less confusing than a multiplicity of strikes.*

LEFT *The parts of this octagonal frame are numbered clockwise to establish a position for each piece.*

2:2
Cutting & fitting

Now that the area to be removed has been measured, marked and identified as waste by hatching, it must be removed. The careful removal of this waste must be considered as important as the joint itself. Slapdash sawing and chipping is a recipe for disaster. The bulk of the waste must be removed efficiently without causing any detrimental effect on the remaining timber.

Sawing, chopping, slicing and drilling are the four processes involved in removing the majority of the waste. The methods used in each case will depend on the joint and its accessibility.

Sawing

Always try to match the saw to the job in hand. If you are cutting *across* the grain, choose a saw that has its teeth ground to a crosscut configuration (see page 15). If, on the other hand, the cut is *with* the grain, the action of teeth ground to a rip profile will speed the work and produce a cleaner cut. Wherever possible, use a backed saw; the steel or brass spine will serve to hold the blade straight as the saw progresses through the wood.

The size of the joint may, however, preclude this: a large tenon may be too long to be cut with a rip-toothed tenon saw, because the back prevents the saw from cutting deep enough. In such a case a short ripsaw may be employed. On smaller joints, smaller saws should be employed. The **gentleman's** (or **gent's**) **saw** is a small backsaw that can be used for finer work. A **dovetail saw** can be used to cut small tenon cheeks. Just because a saw has attracted a common name does not mean it will not cut anything else – a dovetail saw is only a small tenon saw. Both types are available with teeth ground to either crosscut or rip. Indeed, larger dovetails are easier to cut using a larger backsaw – a **tenon saw**.

ABOVE LEFT *Cutting across the grain with a crosscut tenon saw.*

ABOVE RIGHT *The cheeks of smaller tenons are best cut with a rip-toothed tenon saw.*

LEFT *Cutting the cheeks of a larger tenon may require the use of a ripsaw – though this practice is more often associated with construction joinery than furniture building.*

TECHNIQUE:
Sawing vertically

Always cut vertically. With practice, making a saw cut perpendicular to the bench will become second nature. Trying to follow a line that is anything but vertical will feel uncomfortable, and accuracy of cut will deteriorate. Always position the work in the vice so that the cut line is vertical, even if the workpiece itself is not. In the case of dovetails, position the job so that one side of the tail is upright, and make all the cuts for that side; then reposition the job and cut the other side of the tails.

RIGHT *Set the work up to enable vertical saw cuts to be made whenever possible.*

LEFT *Finer crosscut work is carried out with a smaller saw.*

LEFT *A dovetail saw can be used for other joints – here it is cutting the cheeks of a small tenon.*

BELOW *Conversely, a rip tenon saw is being used here to cut the tails of a larger dovetail joint.*

Specialized saws

The relatively 'new kids on the block', as far as the Western craftsman is concerned, are the Japanese pull-saws. These are available in a variety of styles and sizes, and the smaller ones are particularly useful for fine work. The fact that they cut on the pull stroke means that the blade can be made extremely thin, and therefore render a fine cut (kerf). The small *dozuki* saw has a back like a Western dovetail saw, but produces a much finer kerf, which makes it ideal for cutting small dovetails.

Metal-framed saws such as coping and fretsaws are not the most obvious choice of tool for joint cutting, due to their fine blades. Yet, when it comes to removing the bulk of waste between the saw cuts of an end-grain joint, they are invaluable. Which type to choose will depend on the scale of the joint: for large joints a coping saw will do a good job, but for a fine dovetail or finger joint the delicate cut of the jeweller's piecing saw is the best choice.

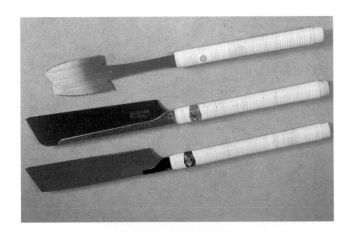

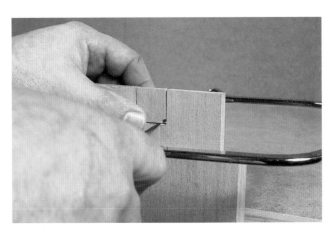

ABOVE LEFT *Japanese saws are making their presence felt. Though they feel strange at first to Western hands, with a little practice their advantages soon become apparent.*

ABOVE RIGHT *Cutting the waste out from between the tongues of a twin tenon with a coping saw.*

LEFT *For delicate work there is nothing to compete with the fine kerf produced by the small dozuki saw.*

Chopping out

Where possible, removing the bulk of the waste with a saw is usually the best option, as minimal stress is imposed on the timber surrounding the joint. Nevertheless, there are times when sawing it away is not a practical option. Cutting the mortise of a mortise and tenon joint is a case in point.

Mortise chisels are designed for heavy work, and have blades that are thicker than they are wide in the smaller sizes. The chisel should be the same width as the mortise to be cut. Using light but positive blows from a mallet, work first from the centre of the joint towards the ends, just breaking

the surface of the timber and severing the grain; stop a little short of the end in order to avoid damaging the edge of the mortise.

Repeat the process with a little more vigour until the required depth is reached. If the chisel is sharp, this process should require the minimum of effort even in the hardest of timbers. The mortise chisel is the thug of chisels and is intended for bulk removal of waste, but removing lots of smaller pieces will result in a much finer finish, and ultimately a better-fitting joint. The final trimming is conducted with a more delicate chisel, without the use of a mallet.

ABOVE *The first stage of chopping the waste from a mortise, starting in the centre and working outwards. This first row of cuts is made to break the grain and establish the area of waste removal.*

LEFT *Although subsequent chopping is carried out with more vigour, there is no need to use excessive force.*

Slicing

Chopping through the fibres of the wood requires short, sharp blows from a mallet. Slicing between the fibres requires a different approach. The halving joint is a good example of where this technique is used. After the shoulders of the joint have been cut with a saw, the waste in the centre is removed with a chisel. Either the square-edged firmer chisel or the more common bevel-edged bench chisel can be used here.

If the area to be removed is wider than the chisel, make some extra relief cuts with the saw to split the area into manageable-sized pieces. These additional saw cuts should be stopped a little short of the line in order to avoid any overcutting.

Starting close to the arris and using hand pressure only, slice away small amounts, cutting at a slight upward angle, steadily progressing down towards the gauged line. Then reverse the material and repeat from the other side. Slice the resultant point of waste flat to the line. The gauged line will prevent break-out, providing you do not cut past it.

TECHNIQUE:
Marking the area to be cut

Prior to chopping out an area, always cut the marked line around the removal area with a marking knife. This will sever the grain and prevent the chopping action from dragging and consequently crushing the fibres of the surrounding area. When a hole needs to be chopped all the way through a piece – as in the case of a through mortise – mark both sides of the timber and remove the waste from both sides through to the centre; this will ensure a clean finish on each side of the joint.

ABOVE *Slicing the waste from a halving joint requires hand pressure alone.*

Drilling

Drilling out the bulk of the waste can save a lot of chopping and reduce the risk of damaging the surrounding material; it can alleviate the pressure on the mating faces of a joint as waste is being chopped out. This technique is particularly useful when establishing a sloping or 'skew' mortise. The bulk of the waste is removed with a hand brace and bit, using a sliding bevel set at the required angle as a guide. The resultant hole can then be finished using chisels and a guide block cut to the required angle.

Where there is a danger of the wood splitting along the grain, drill a hole near where the end of the cut will be, to reduce the risk of the split travelling any further. If a split does occur, it will stop at the hole unless considerable force is applied. You can also use a pillar drill, corded or cordless drill to remove waste.

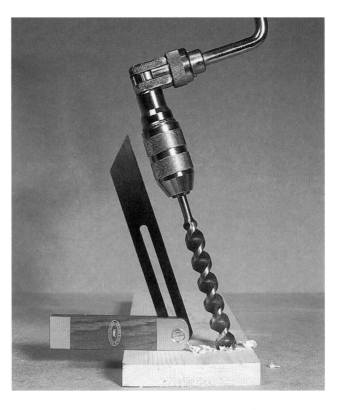

BELOW *There are numerous drill bits available, so make sure you pick the correct one.*

ABOVE *Using a brace and bit to remove the bulk of the waste from an angled mortise. A sliding bevel is used as a visual guide to check the progress of the work.*

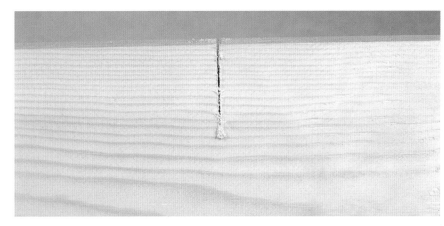

LEFT *Tear-out caused by a saw catching on the fibres of the wood as it exits the cut.*

BELOW *Break-out caused when a plane is passed over unsupported end grain.*

Avoiding break-out

Whatever method of cutting through the wood is used, the cutting tool will be moving in the same direction as it enters and leaves the wood. That may sound obvious, but I highlight this point so as to instil a visual image in your mind of what is happening. The teeth of a saw are slicing or chopping into the wood as they enter, pushing the fibres against the mass of the timber and severing them reasonably cleanly. As they exit the cut, however, there is nothing to prevent the fibres being ripped away from the mass. This will result in a rough, torn finish to the cut. A similar situation will arise with whatever tool is used, if no preventative measures are employed, whether the tool is being passed through the timber or over it (as when a plane is working end grain, for example).

A block of scrap wood can be clamped in place to support the back edge of the cut. Further protection can be afforded by cutting the grain with a knife at the point of exit. But the safest way to avoid break-out is to work from both sides towards the middle, wherever possible.

Additional support

On finer work it may be advisable to add further support to the wood surrounding the material being removed. A cramp applied to either side of a piece that is being mortised will reduce the risk of splitting. When cutting thin material in the vice, a thicker backing piece will prevent the job flexing.

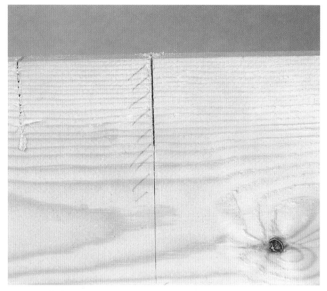

ABOVE LEFT *A block clamped to the workpiece on the 'exit' side will support the end grain and prevent break-out.*

ABOVE RIGHT *A knife cut (as on the right here) will help to eliminate tear-out when sawing.*

LEFT *A cramp is used to support the sides of the timber as it is mortised.*

ABOVE *Backing a thin component with another piece of wood will support it while the joint is cut.*

Getting to it

Sometimes the nature of the joint makes it extremely hard to gain access to its depths in order to clear the waste from the lower corners. Bent or cranked chisels are useful on occasion, as are the skew-ground chisels which allow much better access into a corner. Specialist lock-fitting chisels will also facilitate access to those hard-to-reach places.

Even so, there will come a time when the off-the-shelf tool just will not get the job done. It is at this time that the woodworker turns toolmaker – or at least tool modifier. Old chisels, plane irons and even saw blades are all useful as the raw materials for specialist toolmaking. An old chisel purchased second-hand at a car boot or yard sale can have its sides reground to be a perfect fit between fine dovetails. Old machine-shop hacksaw blades can be used as the raw material for making fine knives or chisels for getting to the bottom of a deep mortise or other joint without obscuring the view. When rigidity is called for, a slice from an old plane iron will make a fine cutting edge that can be used with a fair degree of force.

Final fitting

Once the bulk of the waste has been removed from each component, the joint needs to be fitted. At this stage it will be too tight to assemble. This is because the waste has been removed only *up to* the marked line. If the joint is to fit – and the marking was accurate – the marking line must be split in order for the component parts to fit together. The 'fit' of the joint should be firm and solid-feeling – without any slop, but not requiring excessive force in order

to assemble it. If you like, the parts could be described as being a 'snug' fit. Final trimming can be carried out with nothing more than a sharp chisel. Wider chisels will flatten a wider area and are less likely to dig in. Shaving the inside of a bridle joint is an example of a job where a chisel is the only suitable tool. In other situations, where the joint surfaces are more accessible, it may be easier and more accurate to use a plane.

ABOVE *A twin tenon awaiting final trimming and fitting...*

ABOVE *...and the same joint fitted and ready to assemble.*

Key point

Whatever tool you use it must be sharp, really sharp. 'Really sharp' means a tool that will cut the end grain of softwood cleanly, with a minimum of pressure, and produce a shaving – not just powder. In the case of a plane, it must also be properly adjusted.

FOCUS ON:
Rebate and shoulder planes

Shoulder planes and many rebate planes have their blades bedded at a lower angle than a conventional bench plane, with the bevelled side uppermost. This arrangement gives lots of support to the cutting edge, minimizing any chance of the blade flexing under load and causing the plane to chatter. A traditional shoulder plane has a fixed mouth set extremely tight, and is designed to trim end grain alone. Most rebate planes have an arrangement to adjust the mouth opening – a narrow mouth is necessary when trimming end grain, as opposed to cutting rebates along or across the grain. A further advantage is given when the front of the plane can be removed altogether, thus allowing the tool to be used as a chisel plane. In this configuration the plane can trim right up to a vertical face or into a corner.

The variety of sizes available in rebate and shoulder planes is considerable. Smaller planes can be used in confined spaces, but the larger ones have far greater mass and require less effort to make a clean cut. This makes them ideal for trimming across the grain, as well as trimming end grain.

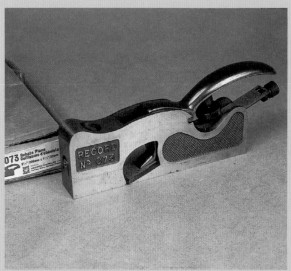

TOP *This dedicated shoulder plane has no mouth adjustment.*

MIDDLE *This type of rebate plane is often referred to as a shoulder plane; it does a great job in both roles, regardless of what you call it.*

BOTTOM *The versatile 3110 plane can be used as a rebate, shoulder, bullnose or chisel plane, as shown on page 18.*

Finishing down to the line

Whatever tools are employed, the trimming must be performed with care and with a methodical approach, constantly monitoring your progress. The last few cuts must be carried out with precise actions, driving the sharpest of tools, to produce as near a perfect finish as possible. If the line you are working to has been made with a traditional marking knife, one side of the cut will be flat and the other bevelled, reflecting the grind of the knife. Assuming the knife has been used correctly, the bevel should be on the waste side, so at the trimming stage the waste material should be removed down to the flat side of the marked line.

If the line was produced with a marking gauge, or with a knife bevelled on both sides, then the trimming must be progressed to the centre of the cut. This will leave a slight chamfer to the edge of the trimmed part. This chamfer is negligible in dimension and is not usually of concern, but in any case it is wise to make gauged lines as fine as possible so as to reduce this effect.

Select one part of the joint to be trimmed and finished to its intended size, ready to receive the other. In some cases the choice of which part to trim is inconsequential, as both parts are similar. When the joint has two distinct parts, it is better to finish the receiving part to size first, and then fit

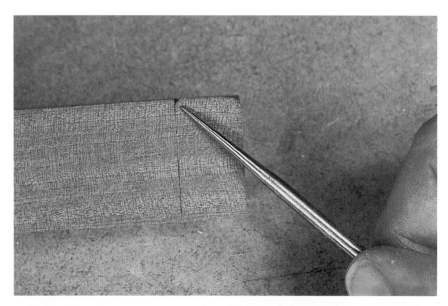

LEFT *Trim to the flat side of the line made by a single-bevelled knife.*

LEFT *When a double-bevelled knife has been used, trim to the centre of the cut line.*

the other part to it. An example of this would be a simple mortise and tenon, where the mortise would be finished to size first and the tenon fitted to it. It is far easier to trim a tenon precisely to size than to try and enlarge a mortise with any finesse.

Trimming

The direction in which the trimming takes place depends on the access. For the most part there will only be one choice. For example, the depth of a notched joint can only be adjusted by trimming across the grain. A tenon could also be trimmed in this manner, but in this case there is another alternative available: as the end of the tenon is open, the tongue could be trimmed along the grain, cutting from the end towards the shoulder. Trimming along the grain can produce a smoother finish. The disadvantage is that the cut will be harder to control, as the chisel may well tend to follow the grain and thereby cut deeper than intended. Another possibility is that the chisel may lift the grain, causing tear-out. It is much better practice to trim across the grain of the tongue with a chisel, or better still a shoulder plane adjusted accordingly.

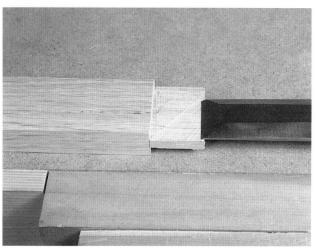

LEFT *Finish the receiving part of the joint – in this case the mortise – and then trim the other part – the tenon – to fit inside it.*

BELOW LEFT *The bottom of a notched joint can only be trimmed across the grain, as the shoulders preclude any other access.*

BELOW RIGHT *Although the tongue of a tenon could be trimmed along the grain...*

RIGHT *...this can cause the chisel to follow the grain, cutting too deeply...*

BELOW LEFT *...and maybe lifting the fibres of the wood, causing tear-out.*

BELOW RIGHT *Trimming across the grain; the rate of removal is easier to control.*

Cutting end grain

Trimming end grain requires a very particular approach. If you imagine the fibres of the wood as a bundle of drinking straws, all stuck together, then the end of the bundle is akin to the end grain. Trying to cut through it, you at first start to crush the straws, until the force exerted is sufficient to cut through them. Once cutting has started, running through the bundle becomes easier, as all the surrounding straws are giving support to the straws being severed. On reaching the other side, the straws at the edge have no support, and are broken away from the bundle rather than cut.

The fibres within the wood behave exactly like the drinking straws. To reduce the crushing of the end grain, not only does the cutting edge need to be sharp, but the finer the angle of cut, the better. Trimming end grain with a chisel – especially one with a fine cutting bevel – will require the minimum of pressure to get started and will make a very fine cut. However, the control of the cut is a little more difficult, so take it easy.

The iron in a conventional metal bench plane is bedded with its bevel facing downwards. Regardless of the angle to which the bevel is ground, the cutting angle will always be the same as the bed or frog

angle of the plane – normally 45°. This arrangement will cut end grain successfully, but considerable force will be required to start the cut and to maintain a steady follow-through. For this reason, the part being trimmed must be properly supported. It is therefore best mounted on a shoot of some kind; the one shown above can double as a bench hook.

For a more delicate approach, the low-angle block plane has its iron bedded at around 13°, with the bevel up. This gives a total cutting angle of only 38° (assuming the iron is ground to a 25° cutting angle), requiring a much lighter force to progress the cut.

TOP *Trimming end grain on an end shoot with a bench plane requires a high degree of force.*

ABOVE *Because of its acute cutting angle, the low-angle block plane requires less force to progress the cut through the end grain.*

One thing these planes cannot do is trim the shoulder of a joint, because the sides of the body prevent the blade from reaching into the corner. The dedicated shoulder plane has a low bedding angle (usually 20°) and a cutting angle on the blade of 25°, giving a total cutting angle of 45°. This is the same angle as on a conventional bench plane; the differences are the exceptionally tight mouth, and the fact that the blade, mounted bevel-up, is supported all the way to the cutting edge.

Designed specifically for end-grain work, this tool does an excellent job when correctly adjusted. A rebate plane with an adjustable mouth, though designed to cut along the grain, can be used as a shoulder plane as well. The Clifton 3110 is such a plane, as its mouth can be adjusted by the removal or insertion of shims. Other, larger adjustable shoulder planes are also useful, as their mass makes the flow across the shoulder easier. Whatever method of removal is being used to trim end grain, the end

LEFT *The dedicated shoulder plane, with its fixed, narrow mouth, is designed to cut end grain cleanly.*

LEFT *The Clifton 3110 can be set up as a small shoulder plane.*

of the cut must be supported. This is usually accomplished by clamping a piece of scrap to the end where the plane leaves the work, as shown on page 76.

Leaving room for glue

Although there should not be any appreciable slack in the joint, the trimming process must allow room for the glue. If the fit is so tight as to scrape the glue off the mating surfaces as it is assembled, the joint will not gain any benefit from the glue. There must be enough room for the glue to form a thin film between the joints. Thin means thin – most of the glues that we use have little or nothing at all in the way of gap-filling qualities (see Chapter 2:3).

When trimming blind joints (that is, joints that do not go all the way through, like stub tenons), there must be enough clearance for the excess glue to escape. Otherwise the joint will not seat properly, due to the hydraulic effect of the trapped glue.

ABOVE *Larger adjustable rebate planes can also be set up as shoulder planes, and their greater mass helps to progress the cut with less effort.*

2:3
Glues, cramps & assembly

Putting a complex piece together can be a rather fraught operation, and the order of assembly must be carefully planned from the start. If the job is to go well, it is essential to choose the appropriate adhesive and to have a suitable assortment of cramps to hand, ready adjusted and laid out in an orderly manner.

Modern glues are easy to use, and produce a bond that in many cases is stronger than the wood itself. The three glues described in this chapter – PVA, polyurethane and powdered resin – are the most commonly used types. There are many other possibilities, from the traditional animal glues to the modern epoxy resins and cyanoacrylate 'superglues'. Although all of these have their uses in woodwork, they are not the domain of the novice, and including them in this brief outline would not do them justice.

Storing adhesives

The method of storage is always advised on the container, and is usually along the lines of 'Store in a cool, dry place out of direct sunlight.' The important thing is to replace the lid properly. In a domestic setting, where the use is far less rapid than in the commercial environment, the glue may well sit around unused for long periods. PVA glues may separate if left standing for a long time, but this is not detrimental and a good stir will usually rectify this.

Shelf life is indicated only as a guide, and to allow manufacturers to limit their liability. Unless you are a prolific woodworker, the chances are that some of your glues will go out of date, but this does not mean that they are no good. Most glues will last far beyond their quoted dates, if stored correctly. If your glue is out of date, try it. If it still works, keep on using it, but be prepared for the day when it won't. More often than not, the structure of the glue will visibly change, making it obvious that it is past its best.

LEFT *The glue can be stronger than the wood itself: here the upper piece of wood has given way, but the joint has not.*

LEFT *PVA or polyvinyl acetate (left) polyurethane (right).*

Regular PVA

The universal woodworker's glue is PVA (polyvinyl acetate), so called after its main constituent. Until recently, ordinary PVA was usually white in the UK but yellow in the US, but during the past few years the American yellow glues have become more readily available in Britain. Rather misleadingly, these yellow PVA glues have been marketed as 'aliphatic resin', giving the impression that they are something entirely different. In fact, many substances can be described as aliphatic resin, including all PVA glues; the yellow glues are just a higher grade of PVA. The yellow colour is not a magic ingredient – it's a dye. All PVA glues will make a satisfactory bond between two correctly prepared pieces of timber, but they differ in working properties and durability.

Open time

The length of time the glue stays workable during a glue-up – referred to as 'open time' – is a large factor in the decision as to which glue to use. Open time can be dramatically affected by atmospheric temperature and humidity. The small print on the bottle will usually give you a guide – a typical figure might be 10 minutes at 20°C (68°F). At higher temperatures the open time may be reduced to a couple of minutes. On the other hand, at lower temperatures – below 5°C (41°F) – the open time will extend to a point where the glue will not properly cure at all.

Fast-curing types are useful when a number of small subassemblies are required to be combined into a larger unit. The glued subassemblies can be removed from the cramps in under an hour, and then put together as a second-stage glue-up without having to wait until the next day. These faster-drying glues generally have better adhesion characteristics in their liquid state (higher initial 'grab') than ordinary PVA.

Glues with a longer open time are invaluable in situations where the glue-up is likely to be complicated. If it is going to take half an hour to coat the job with glue, assemble and cramp it, then you really need a glue with an extended open time – otherwise the first pieces to which you applied the glue will be starting to cure before the cramps are applied, which will greatly weaken the joint.

Waterproof PVA?

There is no such thing as a totally waterproof PVA. Different formulations can result in better resistance to moisture, and some varieties are better than others. Most are labelled 'not suitable for immersion' or something similar. The main use of water-resistant PVA is where the glue joint is open to the weather, but has some additional protection such as paint. External door frames and windows are obvious candidates for this type of glue.

Application of PVA

PVA should be applied as a thin film to both mating surfaces. This can be achieved by using the spout of the bottle, one of the proprietary applicator bottles or a brush. The various makes vary in consistency, and some will spread more easily if slightly thinned with water. Be careful not to over-thin the glue: add a maximum of one part water to 20 parts glue – in other words, 5%, by volume, of water added.

In a perfect world, once the work has been cramped up, a small, continuous bead of glue should be squeezed from the joint along its entire length.

In reality, excess glue is forced out and runs down the vertical surfaces. This can be cleaned off immediately with the use of a damp sponge. Alternatively, after an hour or so, the surplus glue can be pared off with a sharp blade. However, the method I prefer is to sponge away the bulk of the excess glue while it is still in liquid form and then let the joint cure completely before removing the rest with a carbide-tipped paint scraper.

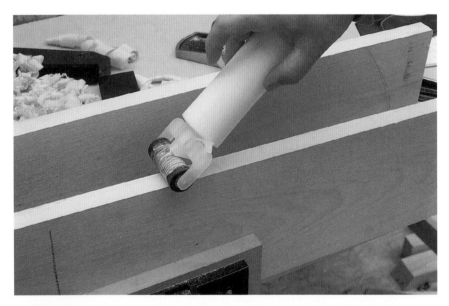

LEFT *PVA can be applied straight from the bottle, with an applicator (as here), or with a brush.*

LEFT *The perfect joint, with just a small bead of glue being squeezed out by the cramps.*

LEFT *Excess glue can be wiped off with a damp sponge...*

LEFT *...or removed with a chisel-shaped knife before it is fully cured.*

LEFT *Fully cured glue can be removed with a carbide paint scraper.*

Polyurethane (PU)

Polyurethane glues are now finding their way into our workshops. They are moisture-cured, taking their requirements from the wood itself or the air around it. In some extreme cases, the surfaces to be joined may need to be moistened with a damp rag in order to activate the curing process. Polyurethane glues are completely waterproof and can be used for exposed external joints, such as in garden furniture.

Application of polyurethane

The glue is applied to one side of the joint only, straight from the bottle. I use a scrap of wood to spread the glue evenly. Try not to get it on your skin – it takes days to wear off. In its uncured state it can be removed with white spirit (mineral spirit), but you have to be quick, because the moisture in your skin starts the curing process immediately. I make a point of wearing disposable skintight gloves if I am doing a large glue-up where I am likely to come in contact with the glue.

As the glue cures it will foam a little at the joints. Let this cure fully and then remove the foam with a sharp blade. Polyurethane glues have a degree of gap-filling ability, but with little or no strength in the fill.

LEFT *Polyurethane glue foams as it cures. Remove the foam with a sharp blade after it has fully cured.*

LEFT *Using a scrap of wood to apply polyurethane glue to one surface only.*

LEFT *Apply resin glue with a brush, but ensure you wash it before the glue cures.*

Powdered resin glues

There are various types, but the best-known is urea-formaldehyde (UF), a powdered glue that was originally developed in the 1930s and represented an advance in technology over the animal glues of the time. It was used mainly in the aviation and boatbuilding industries. It is waterproof and durable when fully cured. Although modern glue technology has negated the need for such a glue in many areas, there are still a good many situations where it can be the answer to a glue-up problem. The trend towards solid wood kitchen work surfaces, for example, means that the installer needs a glue that will hold in the most arduous of situations. Powdered resin is the perfect choice.

Supplied as a powder, it is mixed with water to form a smooth paste. It has good gap-filling properties and the viscosity can be altered during the mixing process. It has a reasonable open time in average conditions, but don't try using it on a summer's day in direct sun – it will cure in the mixing pot before you get the stirring stick out. Please don't ask me how I know this!

Mixing is carried out either by weight or by volume. Do not mix more than you can use before it starts to cure: once the glue starts to set it is of no further use and must be disposed of.

Application of powdered resin glue

I tend to mix powdered glue in an old glass jar and apply it to both surfaces with a brush. As the glue is soluble in water until cured, brushes can be washed in water; the jar may be disposed of after use. Letting the joint 'sit' for a minute or two after application will allow the glue to penetrate the fibres of the wood prior to assembly and final cramping.

Cramps

It does not matter how many cramps you own – another one will always come in handy. The old adage is true: you can never have enough cramps. The more cramps you use, the easier it is to apply an even pressure to the work in hand. With this in mind, for a job I was doing a few years ago in our commercial workshop, I bought 40 Solo cramps to speed the glue-up time – only to find that 42 would have been better!

In the practical world of the home woodworker, where storage space and funds are usually at a premium, a modest selection of cramps has to perform a vast range of tasks. As with all tools, I will always advocate buying the best. However, there are occasions where cheaper cramps will suffice to add some secondary pressure.

The problem with cheap cramps is that they are usually not very solid, and tend to distort under pressure. This can, at best, place an uneven cramping pressure on the joint, and, at worst, distort the joint itself. However, provided the main cramping is done using good-quality cramps, the secondary cramping, to provide added pressure along a joint, can be achieved with lesser-quality cramps. A good example of this would be when assembling a frame with open bridle joints. Good-quality bar cramps are used to square the frame, but cheaper cramps will be adequate to apply pressure to the individual joints.

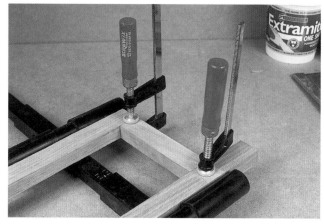

LEFT *Now if only I had some cramps!*

ABOVE *The quality bar cramps are doing the major work, while the cheaper F-cramps apply additional pressure to joints that have already been located.*

OPPOSITE *Spreading the load by means of protective blocks placed between the cramp head and the work. Alternating the cramps above and below the work helps to prevent bowing.*

Spreading the load

To avoid crushing the work it is advisable to spread the load more evenly by cramping an offcut of timber between the face of the cramp and the job. Holding these in place, keeping the parts of the joint together and managing the cramps at the same time can be somewhat challenging. I often use double-sided tape to hold the blocks to the cramps. MDF offcuts are ideal for this; I chop any unwanted long strips into rectangles and fill a bucket with them. They get used for all sorts of other things, too.

RIGHT *MDF squares are ideal for use as protective blocks when cramping. They also have many other uses around the workshop.*

Not too tight!

If the joints have been cut correctly and the component parts are the correct length, the job should assemble without the need to pull anything together. The cramps should be applying just enough pressure to bring the parts into contact and hold them there. If too much pressure is exerted, the glue will be squeezed out and the joint will be weakened. If too little pressure is used, the joint may not seat properly. The correct pressure is enough to hold it but not enough to crush it. The harder the wood, the greater the cramping pressure you can apply without damaging the surface.

Alignment

In its wet state the glue can act as a lubricant, causing the joint to slip as the cramp is tightened. To minimize the risk of this, ensure that the cramp is square to the job and that it is not tending to flex as it is tightened.

When edge-gluing, keeping the boards in line and applying pressure to the outer edges can cause the assembly to slip apart or bow. To rectify this, the bar cramps can be applied alternately above and below the panel. This will equalize the pressure and reduce the distortion problem. To improve the alignment, cauls can be used. These are strips of

LEFT *Careless application of the cramp can cause the joint to slide out of position.*

LEFT *Cauls can be made from timber that has been finished with a slight crown.*

wood that are planed with a slight convexity or 'crown'. Cramping them across the glued-up panel – in pairs, one either side, with the crown facing the panel – will keep all the boards aligned. Apply the bar cramps first, tightened just enough to hold the boards together; then cramp the cauls over the panel and tighten the bar cramps. Newspaper strips under the cauls will prevent them sticking to the panel.

If you are intending to use a lot of glued-up panels, it is worth investing in some panel cramps. The Plano glue press is a good system, and can be built up in stages. It can be hung on the wall to save space – a real asset in a small workshop.

BELOW *Cramp the cauls across the panel to aid alignment and keep the panel flat.*

BOTTOM LEFT *Plano's glue press. The system can be added to, as all parts are available separately...*

BOTTOM RIGHT *...but two cramps will be enough to get you started.*

Avoiding stains

On the subject of protection, there are some other things that should be considered. Some timbers, such as oak and cherry, have high tannin levels. When they come into contact with ferrous metals, black stains can result. Even if the cramping faces are not touching the job, the bars might. Plastic film used for wrapping food can make an effective barrier.

Other forms of staining can occur on lighter wood if the cramps are not clean. Take care of your cramps: if they are showing any signs of rust, deposits of old glue, or oil and grease, do not use them until they have been cleaned. The cramp bars on steel cramps should be as clean as the sole of a plane. A light oiling from time to time, with the surplus removed, will keep them in good condition.

Balancing weight and pressure

Work out the cramping regime and apply the cramps in a logical order – in opposing directions wherever possible. Tighten the cramps so that they stay in place, but wait until they are all in position before final tightening is carried out, working progressively around the assembly.

When cramping one part of an assembly, make sure that you are not putting undue stress on another. The weight of the cramps can cause the assembly to distort if they are all applied from one side; making them face in alternate directions along or around the assembly will even out any twisting effect.

ABOVE LEFT *Using plastic film to prevent the steel bars of the cramps from contacting the job will prevent unsightly staining on woods with a high tannin content.*

ABOVE RIGHT *Regular maintenance of steel cramps is important...*

LEFT *...because rust can soon take hold and transfer to the job.*

TOP *Arranging the cramps to apply an evenly balanced pressure will help to avoid distortion.*

ABOVE *Alternate the cramps so that the weight of the cramps themselves does not cause any stress to the assembly.*

No cramps?

There are many ways of applying pressure to a joint without using the conventional cramps that we tighten with a screw thread. Rubber bands, bungee cord, tyre inner tubes, elastic and luggage straps can all be used to pull a joint together; wedges, string and adhesive tape have their uses too. Or simply trust to gravity, and place a heavy weight on the joint. This can be as light as a tin of beans or as heavy as a length of steel girder – anything that will hold the joint together.

ABOVE *Rubber bands are very useful for holding irregular shapes together.*

ABOVE *Luggage straps can be useful for applying an even closing pressure to a large assembly.*

LEFT *If all else fails, make your own cramp. This frame cramp is ideal for holding all sorts of mitred frames together. It is simply made from hardwood, MDF, dowels and threaded steel rod.*

RIGHT *Stops and wedges are simple but effective.*

RIGHT AND BELOW *These workshop-made bar cramps are simple to make and can supplement the 'real thing'. Wedges driven between the dowels and the work apply even pressure to the joints.*

3

Individual
Joints in Detail

3:1
Butt, edge & mitred joints

3:2
Simple notched & halved joints

3:3
Mortise & tenon joints

3:4
Dovetail joints

3:5
Housing (dado) joints

3:1
Butt, edge & mitred joints

On the face of it, the simplest method of assembling two pieces of wood should be to just stick them together. There are times when this really is all that is needed – edge-jointing boards is a good example. This works because the timber is glued together along the line of the grain, which makes the strongest form of glued joint. However, the edges must be prepared properly. Plane the edges with the longest plane you have. Check your progress with a long straightedge and a try square. The edges must be as straight as possible, and square to the face side – otherwise the joint will be strained and the glue-up may not be flat.

On the other hand, a butt joint in which the ends of two boards are glued together would be the weakest form of joint, with virtually no strength at all. Between these extremes some compromise is available, and there are various ways to effect a serviceable joint.

Making a butt joint

Simply butting the end grain of one piece of wood against the long grain of another, and gluing them together with no other form of mechanical aid, will result in an inferior union between the two pieces. Even if the joint is reinforced in some way – whether it be by using a wooden joining aid such as a dowel or the like, or a metal fixing – the components must still be prepared properly.

Squaring the joint

Flat, square surfaces are what is required. In the joint shown below, the only bearing surfaces are the end of one piece and the edge of the other. If either of these surfaces is not true or square, the error will be magnified by the length of the timber and the joint will be out of true. To avoid this, good preparation is essential. Assuming the timber has been prepared properly (see Chapter 1:2), the sides and edges will be square to each other and should need no further attention. Nevertheless, it is still prudent to check. The end of the joining timber will need cutting and squaring in order to butt up perfectly against the prepared edge.

1 Mark the length to be cut using a sharp pencil and a try square, working from the face edge and side. Mark the waste material by hatching. Confirm the pencil marks with a marking knife.

2 Place the timber on a bench hook with the face side uppermost and the face edge against the hook. Make the cut using a crosscut tenon saw on the waste side of the line. Holding the saw with the index finger pointing along it, use the thumb knuckle of the other hand to align the blade. Make three strokes backwards in order to establish the kerf, then with light pressure progress the cut in the forward direction, making long, positive strokes.

3 Follow the cut line down the far side of the wood and along the top face; start cutting at about a 30° angle, flattening out the cut as the full depth is reached.

4 Check the result using the try square. The joint should be reasonably square in both directions and just outside the cut line. You should strive to get this cut as square as possible – not perfect, just pretty close. Practice makes perfect, and I, for one, am still practising!

5 The next step is to plane the end smooth and square. This can be done in the vice using a block plane, taking all the necessary precautions to prevent breakout, or better still on an end shoot. The butt is now ready for joining, using screws, nails or other fixings, and possibly glue as well.

Mitred joints

Flat mitred joints

Mitred joints are used where it is not desirable to show the end grain of the timber. The mitre also has the advantage of being a halfway house between an edge joint and a butt joint, which enables it to be glued together with a reasonable amount of strength. It is also the easiest solution for joining parts which are moulded, grooved or rebated, as in a picture frame, for example. The angle of the cut depends on the number of sides to be joined; a rectangle, such as a picture frame, will have mitres at 45°. The mitre angle, to which the end of each piece must be cut, is half the overall angle between the intersecting timbers. A square, for example, will have four corners at 90°, so each mitre will need to be cut at 45°.

LEFT *Cutting mitres using a mitre block will save a lot of time, but do not be tempted to skimp on the marking out: the mitre block is only a guide to make it easier to follow the cut lines when sawing at this unnatural angle.*

FOCUS ON:
Mitre angles

The commonest mitre is the 45° variety used to make right-angled structures; but what if you want to make an octagon, for example? Working out the angle at each corner involves the following stages:

1 Divide 360° by the number of corners; this gives 45°, in the case of an octagon.

2 Subtract this figure from 180° to get the internal angle between the two adjacent sides, which for an octagon is 135°.

3 Halve this figure to get the mitre angle of 62.5° for an octagon. This is the angle to which each end of each piece needs to be cut, measuring from the side instead of the end of the workpiece.

Cutting a flat mitre joint is similar to the procedure for cutting a butt joint, except that the cut is made at an angle in both pieces. The end can be planed more easily than a square end, as there is very little risk of breakout so long as the plane moves towards the point of the mitre. A mitre shoot can be made (see pages 112–113) to improve accuracy and to speed up the production of a large number of mitres.

Mitring boxes and carcasses

When mitring the corners of a box across the grain, the marking out needs to be done very carefully if the box is to make up true. Cut the timber for the sides slightly longer than the finished length. On a shallow joint the mitre can be marked from the face edge, marking the angle with the combination square and extending the marks down the face and back. The joint can then be cut and finished as before.

LEFT *Planing the end grain is easier with a mitre than with a square joint; there is no need to protect the end from break-out, so long as you are planing towards the point.*

BELOW LEFT *A mitre shoot will speed up the process and produce a consistent result.*

BELOW RIGHT *Marking the mitre of a shallow box from the face edge. The lines are extended across the face using a square.*

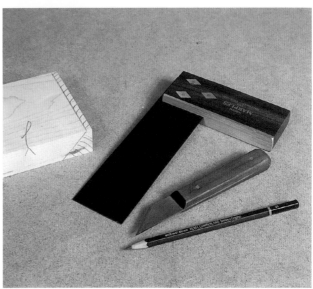

Deeper joints can be marked up in the same manner, although a slight variation in the square or the wood will be vastly exaggerated over the width of the board. To avoid this, the joint can be marked from the end grain. Having cut all the boards to the same length, square each end as if it were a finished face, and check with a long try square. Mark the position of the mitre on the face edge. Now set a cutting gauge to the inner edge of the mitre and scribe a line. Reset the gauge to the outer edge of the mitre and scribe a second line. Repeat for each board.

Cut the mitre with a crosscut tenon saw, or handsaw if the joint is too deep. The cut should be made just inside the waste, leaving a small amount of material to be planed off on the appropriate mitre shoot.

LEFT *Wider joints are marked from the end, using a cutting gauge. The end must be cut square and accurately finished, so that the stock of the gauge is registering on a true surface.*

BELOW *Remove the waste using a tenon saw or a crosscut handsaw, depending on the depth of the joint, leaving a small amount of material proud of the line.*

Long-grain mitres are usually marked up using a conventional marking gauge, and are then planed to the correct angle after the board has been ripped to a width slightly greater than required. It is not worth trying to rip the board at 45° to begin with, since the removal of the waste by planing is a relatively easy job, especially when a donkey's-ear mitre shoot is available (see page 113).

BELOW *Trimming the joint on a donkey's-ear shoot.*

BELOW LEFT *Marking the position of a long-grain mitre. The widest dimension is marked from the face edge onto the face side...*

BELOW RIGHT *...and the incline of the mitre is then marked on each end of the board and the waste identified by hatching.*

RIGHT *Excess timber is removed using a ripsaw. There is no need to try and rip to the mitre angle, as shooting with the grain is easy going and will produce a good mitre very quickly, even from a square edge.*

BELOW LEFT *Align the marks on the edge of an angled shoot and clamp the board firmly in place. A stop at the end will relieve shear force from the cramps and prevent the board from slipping.*

BELOW RIGHT *Shoot down to the line. The shoot should stop you planing any further, but keep an eye on the mark just in case something is adrift.*

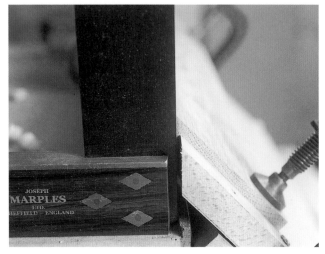

Mitre shoots

A mitre shoot is basically a jig designed to present a piece of timber to the sole of the plane at a given angle. There are many ways to accomplish this, and the design of the shoot will vary according to the position of the mitre on the workpiece. Three of the most common forms are described here. In each case the mitre angle is usually set at 45°, but other angles can be made as required.

End mitre shoot The end mitre shoot consists of a baseboard made from 18mm ($^{23}/_{32}$in) MDF. To this is laminated a second piece of MDF which has been fitted with a hardwood edge to form a running face for the plane. At the midpoint a pair of stops are added at +45° and −45° to the running face. Great

care should be taken while building this kind of shoot, as any error will be transferred to every mitre finished on it.

When the wood is of rectangular section, both ends can be shot from the same end of the mitre shoot. However, when a moulding or strip with an irregular cross section is mitred, the left- and right-hand mitres are shot from opposite ends of the shoot, by either pushing or pulling the plane as appropriate.

Box mitre shoot If the cross section of the mitre is greater than the width of the plane iron, it is too large to be shot on an end shoot. In this case a box mitre shoot is used. This, again, can be built from 18mm ($^{23}/_{32}$in) MDF with running faces made from

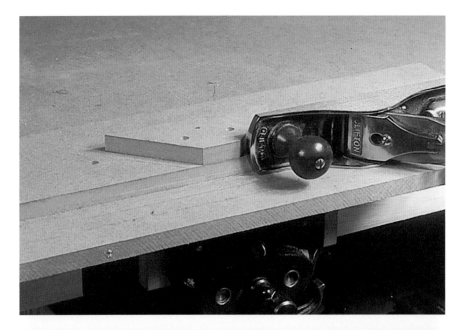

LEFT *End mitre shoot.*

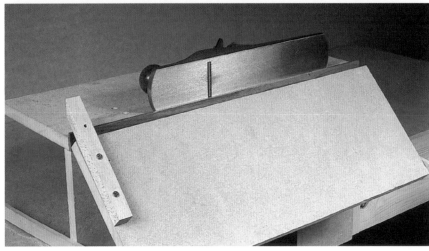

LEFT *Donkey's-ear shoot.*

applied hardwood strips. The piece being shot is held in position using cramps passing through holes cut in the side of the box; the same cramps can also fix the box to the end of the bench. If this is not practical, the piece can be held firm using wedges and spacers inside the box. The mitre is shot using the hardwood trims on the box as a guide, and the corner as a stop. Care is required not to damage the reference faces.

Donkey's-ear shoot Long mitres are shot on a donkey's-ear shoot. This is a board set at (usually) 45° to a vertical board which is either secured in a vice or clamped to the skirt of the bench. The angled board has a stop attached to it, which takes in the profile of the board being shot and somewhat

resembles a donkey's ear – hence the strange name. End-grain mitres are shot with the stop, or donkey's ear, positioned in the centre of the board; this enables both ends to be shot with the face edge against the stop. The first end is shot with the workpiece against the stop and the plane pushed across the mitre. The other end is shot by placing the piece against the *back* of the stop, with the plane pulled across the mitre.

3:2
Simple notched & halved joints

Where strength is required, it is necessary to move on from merely butting or mitring joints together. A picture frame is, by definition, a mainly decorative object that requires little strength – just enough to hold the picture and the glass. The mitres are usually strengthened with a mechanical fixing, just to be sure. However, the bottom line is that there is no inherent strength in joints of this kind. Butt and mitre joints rely totally on outside forces to maintain their relationship to each other – without glue or mechanical fixing they will simply fall apart.

The next step up the development ladder is to the halved or notched joints. Their design locks the components together by recessing the full width of each component into the other, by half the depth of the wood. Used flat, for example, this method of jointing can be used as a face frame for a cupboard. Used upright, it can be used to make the intersections between the dividers in a compartmented box or drawer. There are many other uses for this kind of joint.

Notched joints

A notched joint is where the full thickness of one piece of timber is let in or 'notched' into another, so that one component is supported, at least in part, by a shoulder formed in the other. The simplicity of this joint makes it ideal for use in construction, and it has many forms. Because it is generally used in conjunction with a mechanical fixing, it only just falls within the scope of this book. A development of the notched joint is the halved or halving joint, which is really a double-notched joint, if you like.

Halving joints

Halving joints, although simple, need to be cut with greater care than you would expect. Any gaps or imperfections will show, as most of the cut edges are visible from one side or the other. More often than not the requirement is for a 90º intersection between the component parts. However, this is not always the case: this is an easy method of joining polygonal shapes together without having to cut complicated joints.

Halving joints fall into in three types: end-to-end halving, cross-halving and T-halving. Cutting these joints is an exercise in marking from one component to another.

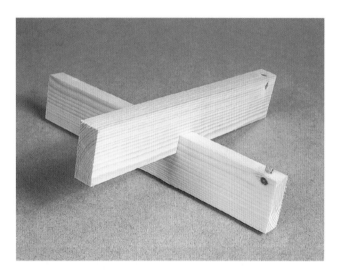

ABOVE LEFT *A notched joint provides support. One component is notched, usually to accept the full thickness of the other.*

ABOVE RIGHT *Variations on a theme: halving joints can be made at any angle.*

LEFT *There are three basic types of halving joint: end-halving, cross-halving and T-halving.*

Making an end-halving joint

1 Make sure that the components are matched face side to face side. Starting with the piece that will be cut away on the face side, mark the shoulder line, slightly further from the end than the width of the other component.

2 Set a marking gauge to the approximate midpoint of the timber's thickness. With the stock against the face side, mark a dot with the point of the gauge.

FOCUS ON:
End-halving joints

Theoretically, if the stock is of similar dimensions the two parts of this joint should be identical, and with practice that should be possible to achieve. Having said that, it is not as important to get the components identical as it is to get a really good, crisp fit. Obviously the first part should be cut as near perfectly as possible; but the second component must then be cut to fit the first. If that means that the parts are slightly different in dimension, so be it. So long as the difference is small, it will not show.

3 Now, keeping the gauge setting the same as before, make a second dot with the stock on the other face.

4 If the two dots coincide, the gauge is set at the midpoint. If it is not, there will be a gap between the dots; adjust the gauge accordingly. By holding the stock of the gauge and *lightly* tapping the shaft on the benchtop, the setting can be adjusted until the midpoint is found. You know you have found it when the pin falls into the same dot when gauged from either side of the timber.

5 Now, with the stock registering on the face side, lightly scribe a line around the end of the timber.

6 Project the shoulder line down each edge until it intersects with the gauge line.

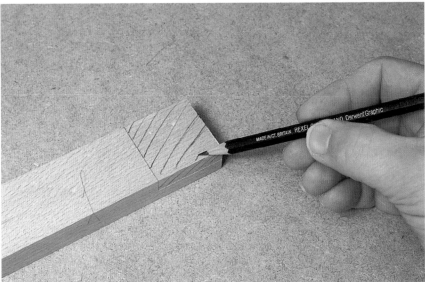

7 Mark the area to be removed as waste.

8 Cut the shoulder down to the gauged line using a small tenon or gentleman's saw, just outside the line on the waste side.

9 Now set the timber in the vice at about 45° so that you can see both the cheek lines, and saw down to the shoulder line, preferably using a saw with its teeth sharpened to a rip profile. Continue cutting, steadily lowering the handle, until the two cuts meet, at which point the waste will fall away free.

10 Clean the joint, back to the centre of the scribed line, using a sharp, wide chisel. Alternatively, an adjustable-mouth shoulder or rebate plane can be used with the mouth set fairly wide to prevent it from becoming clogged.

11 The shoulder should be pared back to the cut line with a chisel; or the shoulder plane can be used, set fine, so long as a piece of scrap is cramped on at the end of the shoulder to prevent break-out.

12 The first piece is now finished, and, after ensuring that all the faces are true and square, it should not be trimmed any further.

13 Using the first half of the joint as a guide, mark up the second piece of timber – still referencing the gauge against the face side – and cut the waste away in a similar manner to the first.

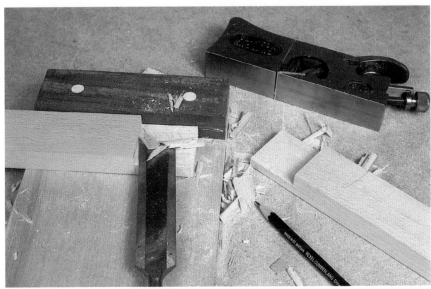

14 This time, trim the joint by constant trial and error so that it fits the first part exactly, removing small amounts of material at a time until the fit is perfect.

15 The chances are that the parts will vary slightly, so mark each joint as a matched pair to ensure that they will be paired correctly at the glue-up stage. Mark them with letters or numbers, or with simple witness marks, as here.

Making a cross-halving joint

1 Mark the position of the first shoulder on one component, squaring a line across the face side using a try square.

2 Mark the position of the second shoulder using the intersecting component as a guide...

FOCUS ON:
Cross-halving joints

A cross-halving joint is where the two components pass through each other, both on the same plane. Again, in theory, both halves of the joint should be identical, but for a perfect result it is better to fit one part to the other, rather than attempt to make two identical pieces independently.

3 ...and again square the line across the face.

4 Gauge the depth of the halving from the face side onto each edge, and square the shoulder lines down the edge to meet the gauged depth.

5 Hatch the waste area, and confirm the lines with a marking knife as usual.

Next, using a tenon or gentleman's saw and a bench hook, cut the shoulders on the waste side of the cut lines down to the gauged depth. The waste now has to be removed with a chisel, as there is no access for a saw. On a wide halving it may be easier to split the waste into smaller sections by making additional saw cuts.

6 Secure the timber so that the gauge line is above the vice jaws. With a sharp chisel, bevel down, pare away the waste using firm hand pressure. A *gentle* tap with the palm of the hand is all that should be necessary, more for control purposes than to propel the chisel. Remove the waste from the top edge to just above the gauge line so as to form a ramp. Turn the timber around in the vice and repeat, forming a second ramp in the opposite direction.

7 Now turn the chisel over and start to flatten the bottom down to the gauge line on both edges.

8 Using a wide chisel, trim the shoulders to fit the other component. This can be done by eye, or a block can be used, as shown here, to keep the chisel square. Remove small slivers, continually checking your progress against the other component. The second part of the joint is cut in a similar manner, taking all the critical dimensions from the part already completed. Careful fitting and trimming will result in a well-fitting joint.

FOCUS ON:
T-halving joints

When a joint is made part-way along one member to receive the end of another, the two components of the joint are not identical. This joint is a combination of the end-halving and cross-halving joints already described and is cut using these techniques. It is better to cut and finish the end joint first, and use this as a guide to mark the other part.

Further strength can be added to the T-halving joint by dovetailing it. This form is often used to prevent components of a piece spreading; the rails of a long table or the carcass of a chest are places where it could be used. It is simply a matter of

setting the shoulders of the receiving part at a converging angle, rather than parallel. The angle of convergence will depend on the timber being used (see Chapter 3:4).

The other part is marked as for an end halving, except that the edge cut lines are extended down the whole depth of the sides to allow the shoulders of the dovetail to be cut. The dovetail is cut using a rip-toothed saw, with the component held in the vice so that the cut is perpendicular to the bench top. Trimming and fitting is carried out using a chisel, as for the normal T-halving.

ABOVE *A T-halving joint.*

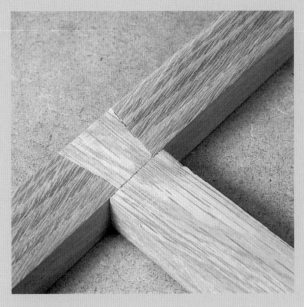

ABOVE *A variation on the T-halving joint is the dovetailed T-halving. The dovetail adds mechanical strength to the joint in tension.*

3:3

Mortise & tenon joints

The mortise and tenon joint, in all its various forms, is used more than all the other forms of joints grouped together. It can be an ultra-fine joint, used to assemble delicate fine furniture, or a massive lump of a joint in an oak-framed building. Regardless of size, it must be constructed with care if it is to be successful.

The techniques used to produce mortise and tenon joints are the same, whatever the scale; only the size of the tools will change.

There are dozens, if not hundreds, of variations on the mortise and tenon, all with a common basic form: a cross-grain hole (mortise) into which a long-grain tongue (tenon) is inserted. The hole may go all the way through, or be 'blind'; it may even be partially open at one end, in the case of a haunched tenon. A mortise completely open at one end has been known by many names – an open mortise or a slot mortise, to mention but two. I call it a bridle joint.

The tenon can be shouldered on one side (barefaced) or two sides, be reduced in width on one or both edges, have a step (haunch) formed in it to fit a groove or resist twisting, or be doubled or quadrupled. Whatever form the joint takes, the same basic cutting and fitting method applies.

FOCUS ON:
Proportion

When the pieces to be joined are of equal thickness, the tenon (and therefore the mortise also) should be made one third the thickness of the stock. Any wider than this, and the sides of the mortise will become too thin to support any sideways thrust of the tenon. Conversely, if the tenon is too thin there is a danger that it may break off at the shoulders when stressed.

When the mortise is to be cut into larger stock than the tenon, you can afford to make the tenon proportionally thicker, so long as the one-third rule is not broken in regard to the mortised component.

Ideally, the width of a tenon should not exceed five times its thickness. If a wider joint is required, twin tenons are advisable.

The length of the tenon depends on the type of joint required, but in typical applications, a stopped mortise and tenon joint needs to penetrate the wood between half and two thirds of its total depth, to maintain strength.

Following these rules of proportion is the ideal whenever possible, but it is not always feasible. If for some aesthetic or physical reason the recommended proportions cannot be adhered to, common sense must prevail.

Marking and cutting a stopped mortise

1 The first thing to do is to mark the position and length of the mortise, using a pencil and a square.

2 Select the mortise chisel that is closest to one third the width of the timber, and set the pins of your mortise gauge to the width of the chisel.

3 To centre the pins on the timber, set the stock of the gauge to where you judge the centre to be, and mark the timber from the face side. Then turn the mortise gauge around and mark from the other side. If the pins are centred, the marks will coincide. If not, adjust the stock of the gauge until they do.

4 Once the mortise gauge has been centred on the stock, scribe a pair of lines to run between the pencil marks. Cut in the pencil lines with a knife to confirm the length of the mortise.

5 Mark the required depth of the mortise on the blade of the chisel using masking tape; allow a fraction extra for clearance beyond the end of the tenon.

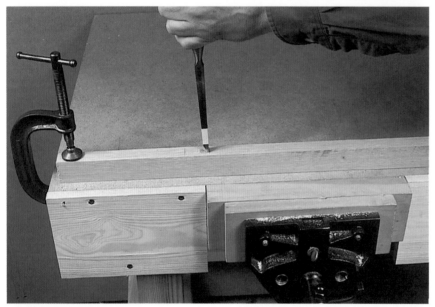

6 Remove the waste material, starting in the middle of the mortise, by chopping small amounts of material at a time and moving back in stages towards the cut line. Stop short of the line – the remaining waste will be removed in the final stages. Leaving it there until the bulk of the work is done will protect the edge of the mortise from being crushed as you lever out the cut waste.

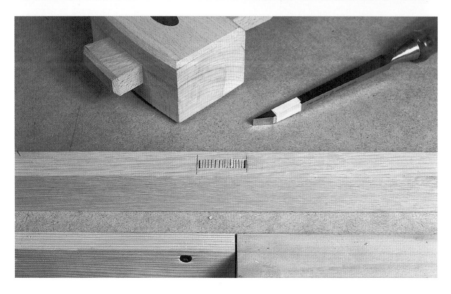

7 Now turn the chisel round and repeat the same process for the other half of the mortise. Continue this process until the desired depth is accomplished.

8 The chopping action will tend to eject the chips as the chisel cuts deeper.

9 The remaining material is levered out.

10 Finish the mortise by smoothing the sides with a wide, sharp chisel.

11 Trimming the ends back to the cut line with the mortise chisel.

12 Scrape the mortise chisel along the bottom to smooth out any remaining imperfections.

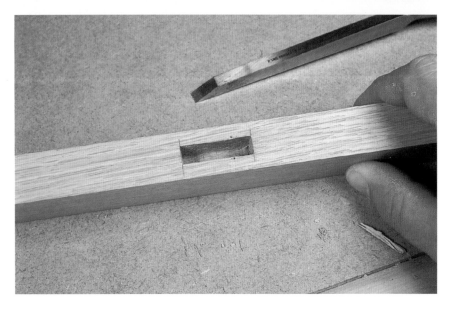

13 The finished stopped mortise.

Making a through mortise

A mortise that is intended to pass right through the timber is called a through mortise. It is made in the same way as a stopped mortise, except that the work is carried out from both sides.

The pencil lines are extended around the timber to the other side, and the mortise gauge is used on both sides to scribe the thickness of the mortise. Care must be taken to ensure that the marking is accurate, if the two halves are to align. Remember always to use the face side as a reference for the square and the mortise gauge.

TECHNIQUE:
Gauging

Don't let the gauge lines run past the ends of the mortise, as this will spoil the look of the joint. One way to avoid this is to stab the points of the gauge into the wood first, at the place where you want the gauge marks to stop. Then gauge slowly and gently so that, as the gauge approaches the end of the mortise, the pins fall into these stab marks and stop the gauge in its tracks.

Key point

Remember not to change the setting of the mortise gauge until you have marked all your mortises and all your tenons.

ABOVE *Extending the marking around the workpiece for a through mortise.*

ABOVE *The finished through mortise.*

Marking and cutting the tenon

1 Mark the position of the shoulders of the tenon with a pencil and square.

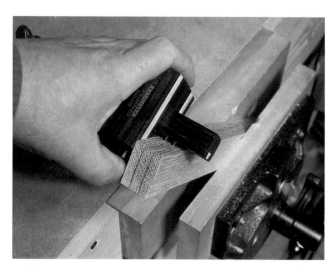

2 The points of the mortise gauge must be set to the same width as the mortise. Check that they are still centred – if the timber is the same dimension as that used for the mortise, they should be. Scribe a pair of lines around the end of the timber, from the shoulder line on one edge to the shoulder line on the other.

3 Use a marking knife to confirm the pencil lines. Hatch the waste with a soft pencil.

4 Set the timber in the vice at about 45° so that you can see the gauge lines on both side and end. Working on the waste side of the line, start to cut the cheeks of the tenon until you reach the shoulder line.

5 Then reset the timber in the vice and cut down to the shoulder line on the other edge. It is best to use a backsaw with rip-set teeth. Take care not to overcut the shoulder, as any saw cuts that extend beyond the line will show when the joint is assembled.

6 Remove the timber from the vice and set it on the bench hook to cut the shoulders. Cut on the waste side of the line, this time using a crosscut backsaw. Once the cut has been started, drop the handle of the saw down until the blade is parallel and carefully cut down the shoulder line until the waste falls away. Square the shoulders down to the cut line using a chisel or shoulder plane (see Chapter 2:2).

7 The tenon cheeks are trimmed down to fit the mortise at the fitting stage.

Variations on a theme

The first refinement is to add **cosmetic shoulders** to the edges of the tenon in order to hide the point at which the tenon engages the mortise completely. These additional shoulders add no significant strength to the joint but will cover any misfit. This technique should not be used as an excuse for bad workmanship, otherwise the joint will be compromised. Cutting and trimming of the cosmetic shoulders must be completed with extra care to ensure that they align accurately with the constructional shoulders. Remember to saw the cheeks on all four sides before cutting the shoulders, so as not to cut away your marking out.

Going the other way, single-shouldered tenons, known as **barefaced tenons**, are sometimes used where access is limited or where adjacent tenons might clash – on a table leg, for example. In this case the tenon should be no less than half the thickness of the stock it is cut from.

When a mortise and tenon joint is employed at the extreme end of a frame member, it may not be desirable for the side of the tenon to be exposed (which would convert the joint into a bridle joint). Simply reducing its width will be enough to conceal it and prevent it turning out of the open mortise; but the narrower the tenon, the less resistance the joint

ABOVE *Cosmetic shoulders to conceal the joint.*

ABOVE *Square-haunched tenon.*

ABOVE *Barefaced tenon.*

ABOVE *Triangular-haunched tenon.*

will have to twisting. This problem can be alleviated by adding a step or **haunch** to the side of the tenon and cutting a corresponding socket alongside the mortise. The haunch can be square – in which case it will show on the outside – or you can use a triangular haunch that does not break the surface, making a cosmetically superior joint. Haunches are also added to tenons, when they are used in panel and frame construction, in order to fill the visible groove at the end of a stile.

If the joint is too wide for a single tenon to be used and still follow the rules of proportion, use twin tenons – two tenons one above the other, joined by

a web that is about a quarter the length of the tenon. The twin mortises are cut separately, then the recess for the web is cut between them.

If the wood is too thick for a single tenon, the joint is doubled. Two tenons and two mortises are cut next to each other to form a double joint. In this case there is no web between the tenons. The usual proportions are maintained, except that the central shoulder is common to both tenons; this means that each tenon and shoulder should be one fifth the thickness of the workpiece. The waste between the two tenons is chopped out with a chisel.

ABOVE *A haunched tenon used to fill the exposed groove in panel and frame construction.*

ABOVE *Double tenons are used when the stock is thick.*

ABOVE *Twin tenons are used for wide joints.*

ABOVE *Marking up the material for the wedges.*

ABOVE *Sawing the wedges from the stock.*

Wedged tenons

Wedged through tenons are mostly used in doors
and window frames, for joints which may be exposed
to changing conditions. The mortise is cut with a
narrower opening on the shoulder side than on the
exposed side; the wedges expand the tenon so that it
takes on a dovetail shape, making it impossible for it
to pass back through the mortise. Wedges can also be
used to add strength in furniture, and if a contrasting
wood is used they become a design feature as well.

If wedges are added to a stopped tenon it becomes
a **fox** or **fox-wedged tenon**; the bottom of the
mortise drives the wedges home as the joint is
assembled. The mortise must, of course, be cut to
accommodate the expansion of the tenon that the
wedges will cause. This makes it almost impossible
for the joint to be dismantled, with or without glue.

The size and angle of the wedges will vary
according to the material and the type of joint being
constructed. A slope of 1 : 8 (around 7°) is the ideal in
hardwoods. A steeper slope of say 1 : 6 (around 9.5°)
should be adopted for softwood.

Cutting wedges

The wedges should be cut with the same amount of
care as when cutting the joint itself. Prepare a piece
of timber of similar thickness to the tenon, and mark
out the wedges across the end. Having decided
on the required slope, mark the length accordingly:
for example, a wedge in 1 : 8 ratio that was 48mm
long would be 6mm wide at the thickest point; if 2in
long, the thick end would be ¼in.

To cut wedges of any given length, start by
marking a square line across the timber from the
face edge, at the appropriate distance from the end
of the timber. Mark the thickness of the wedges,
including an allowance for the thickness of the saw
cuts, then bisect these rectangles diagonally to
produce opposed pairs of wedges.

Set the timber in the bench vice so that the slope
of the wedge is vertical. Using a fine saw – a dovetail
saw is ideal – cut all the slopes. Then reposition the
timber so that the marks between the wedges are
vertical, and proceed to cut and remove every other

LEFT *Planing the wedges, using a block plane held in the vice and a push stick to protect your fingers.*

LEFT *The tenon cut to receive the wedges.*

wedge. The wedges still attached to the timber are now removed by crosscutting on the bench hook. To plane the wedges smooth, secure a fine-set block plane in the bench vice with its sole uppermost. Using a miniature push stick – or a pencil eraser will do – the wedge can be planed smooth. One or two passes should be all that is required. The wedges are usually placed around one fifth of the way in from each end of the tenon; on a very large tenon, four wedges might be needed.

LEFT *A guide block cut to the required angle is used to steer the chisel when sloping the ends of the mortise.*

LEFT *Assembling the wedged tenon.*

Cutting the flared mortise

In order to accommodate the expansion of the tenon when the wedges are driven home, each end of the mortise must be angled at a similar slope to that of the wedges. Cut a conventional through mortise to start with, then open it out from the exposed side to make room for the wedges. Use a guide block at the required slope, made from an offcut, to guide the chisel. Start cutting from the edge of the mortise, working back towards the new width line. Take care not to enlarge the mortise on the shoulder side of the joint.

When assembling the joint, drive each wedge alternately, and stop when the tenon has expanded enough to fill the mortise. In the case of a stopped

mortise that is going to receive a fox-wedged tenon, the bottom of the mortise must be opened out, working from the narrow end. This is done using a guide block as before, except that the negative slope makes the handling of the chisel feel awkward if the trimming is carried out on the benchtop. Clamping the timber in the vice at an angle greater than the slope will make the job easier.

The length of a wedge for a through tenon is not critical, as any excess material can be removed after the joint is assembled. This is not the case with a foxed tenon: the wedges must be exactly the right length to expand the tenon without hindering its travel into the mortise.

Pegged and pinned joints

Most of the following joints owe their existence to the historical need to assemble a strong joint with inadequate or non-existent glues. With today's glue technology these joints are used, more often than not, for their appearance, especially in furniture.

One area where they are still used today, to great effect, is in the construction of traditional timber-framed buildings. Huge joints are cut into immense timbers with great precision. This is usually done off-site, prior to assembly at the building site where all the parts are finally put together and the pegs are driven home to hold everything in place. These joints are nothing more than scaled-up versions of the joints shown in these pages.

The one thing that all these joints have in common is that they are held in place with the addition of a wooden pin or peg. The pin can be used to draw or hold the joint tight, or it can simply be added after assembly to lock the joint together and prevent any subsequent movement.

The **tusk tenon** is a through tenon that is longer than the thickness of the timber that it is passing through. The tenon has a square hole cut through it that does not fully emerge through the mortise. This allows the joint to be pulled together by inserting a wedge-shaped key into the hole. The joint can be taken apart, and it has therefore been used for centuries to build knock-down furniture.

ABOVE *Cutaway view of a foxed tenon.*

A **drawn** or **drawbored tenon** is any type of tenon that is drawn together using a tapered pin. The joint is made using the standard method of construction, then a hole, or a pair of holes, is bored through the mortise. It is advisable to insert a piece of scrap in the mortise while drilling, to prevent break-out on the inside of the cheek.

The tenon is then inserted and pushed home. Using a pencil, the position of the hole is marked onto the tenon, through the hole already bored in the mortised component. A similar-sized hole is then drilled through the tenon, but slightly nearer the shoulder, so that when the joint is reassembled the holes in mortise and tenon are misaligned.

A dowel, of a similar diameter to that of the hole, is sharpened slightly at one end and driven through the hole in the mortise. On entering the offset hole in the tenon, the dowel will pull the tenon further into the mortise. Trial and error will indicate the amount of offset required, but it need only be slight to be effective. This sort of joint is most useful where excessive racking or seasonal movement is expected; garden furniture would be a case in point.

Finally, pegged joints can be used as an additional security, to hold the joint together in case an extraordinary strain is applied. The joint is again made in the normal fashion, but this time it is glued and cramped together before a hole is bored through the assembled joint and a dowel peg is glued in place. A classic use of this joint is to be found in chair construction, where seat components are joined to the legs.

ABOVE LEFT *A tusk tenon used to secure the stretcher between the splayed ends of a stool.*

ABOVE RIGHT *The square hole in the tusk tenon is positioned so that the key will pull the joint together as it is driven home.*

LEFT *The holes through a drawn tenon and its mortise are purposely misaligned.*

LEFT *The peg is tapered at the leading end.*

LEFT *The peg tightens the joint as it is driven home.*

LEFT *The peg is finally trimmed flush with the face of the joint.*

3:4
Dovetail joints

Probably the most famous of all woodworking joints, the dovetail is surrounded with an air of quality and tradition. In the days before modern glues, a joint had to supply mechanical strength in order to resist the stresses put on it. The dovetail does this by locking the wedge-shaped 'tails' into matching sockets.

Various types of dovetail joint have developed over time, from the common single-dovetail frame joint to the sophistication of the secret mitred dovetail, hidden behind the faces of a mitre where it is never to be seen. This complex joint owes its origin to the fact that animal glues had limited strength, and hiding the 'mechanics' inside the wood meant that a continuous outside face could be maintained.

Cutting dovetails is no more difficult than cutting any other joint. In fact, it can be more forgiving than some – a slight error in cutting may not show once the joint is assembled. Having said that, I am certainly not advocating bad practice. A badly cut joint will not only look bad, but will be more likely to fail.

LEFT *Machine-cut dovetails: functional but devoid of character.*

Design

There are three things to consider when designing a dovetail joint: strength, aesthetics and economy of labour. Strength can be determined by the number of joints, the steepness of the dovetail angle and the wood being used. Aesthetics is all about number and proportion, and whether the tails are to be seen as a 'feature' or as a subtle presence. The angle of the tails is dictated by both of these considerations, balanced against the strength of the wood being used.

Strength

The type of timber used has a bearing on the slope of the tails. The slope is usually measured in the form of a gradient, such as 1 : 6. This means that for each six units of travel the slope will rise one unit. The smaller the number, the steeper the joint. As a general rule, joints in softer woods are made steeper than those in harder woods. A good starting point would be to use 1 : 6 in pine and 1 : 8 in oak, but these gradients or ratios are not set in stone as a sort of unbreakable rule.

Aesthetics

Getting the proportions right will not only make the job look better, but will enhance the strength of the joint. The majority of dovetail joints seen on furniture today are machine-made. The monotonous regularity of such joints takes the soul out of the piece. More often than not, this mechanical regularity, enforced by the soulless mathematics of the machine, can make the piece look completely lifeless and merely functional.

Economy of labour

There is no point in making work for yourself just for the sake of it. Take a look at an old, traditionally made drawer from a chest, for example. Assuming it has been assembled with dovetails, the side where the front of the drawer is fixed will show several nicely finished, fairly substantial dovetails locking the face of the drawer to the sides. This joint has to be strong enough to pull the drawer and its contents out of the chest. If you remove the drawer, however, you will most likely see that the back has been joined with a minimum of effort. If there are dovetails, they will likely be very fine and few in number. This is acceptable because of the minimal amount of stress that will be endured by this joint.

Through dovetails

There are two components to a dovetail joint. The part that looks like the tail of a dove is, not surprisingly, called the **tail**. On the other component, the pieces that fit between the tails are called the **pins**. A through dovetail is one in which the end grain of both tails and pins is exposed on the outside.

The relationship between tails and pins is infinitely variable, which can make the whole task seem daunting to the uninitiated. Some of these variations are for reasons of strength, others for design and some are pure showmanship. Even spacing, as in the exercise below, is the theoretical optimum as far as strength is concerned, but this is one of those subjects that can keep me talking all afternoon.

The angle of slope will also affect the strength of the joint: too shallow and you will be making a finger joint, too steep and you increase the risk of splitting the grain of the pins or tails during assembly. I tend to favour the traditional guidelines mentioned earlier – 1 : 6 for softwood and 1 : 7 or 1 : 8 for hardwood.

Marking out

There are plenty of proprietary gauges, templates and 'squares' set at various angles that are designed to aid the marking of the slope. The most versatile tool to use, however, is the sliding bevel. Let us assume that a joint is to be cut in hardwood and the slope ratio adopted is 1 : 7.

ABOVE *These are the tails of the joint.*

ABOVE *These are the pins of the joint.*

Making a through dovetail joint

1 Using a square, mark a line on a scrap piece of board, perpendicular to one edge. Mark off seven equal units – inches, centimetres, whatever you prefer. Next, mark a point one unit away from the perpendicular line on the edge of the board. From this point, scribe a line to the seven-unit mark on the perpendicular line. This new line inclines at a ratio of 1 : 7 to the edge of the board.

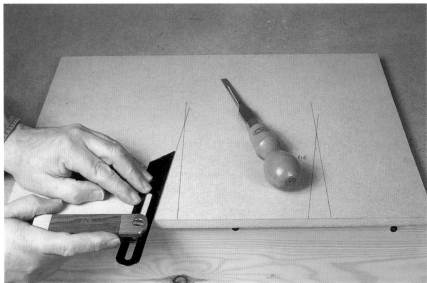

2 Set the stock of the sliding bevel against the edge of the board and align the blade with the drawn slope. Use this setting to mark the slope of your dovetails.

3 Set a cutting gauge to the thickness of the material that will have the pins cut into it, and mark this distance across the end of the piece that is to form the tails, on the face side. This line will determine the length of the tails.

4 Using a square and a sharp pencil, draw a line halfway between the gauged line and the end of the workpiece. This line will be divided up into units and used as a reference for marking the slopes of the tails.

5 Decide upon the number of tails required. For this example the timber is 110mm wide and we want two tails. At each end of the joint the pins are narrower in order to give a pleasing appearance. The joint will therefore contain two tails, one full pin and two partial pins. If the tails and full pin are 26mm wide at their halfway point, the narrower pins at each end will be 16mm wide, again at the midpoint. So, mark from one end as follows: 16, 26, 26, 26mm; this will leave a further 16mm to the other end.

(If you prefer imperial measurements, make the tails and full pin 1in wide and the part pins ⅝in, giving an overall width of 4¼in. Mark from one end: ⅝, 1⅝, 2⅝, 3⅝in, leaving ⅝in to the other end. Do not mix metric and imperial measurements, as the equivalents are not quite exact.)

6 Using the sliding bevel, mark the first slope from the first point on the line. Then the second slope is marked in the opposite direction from the next point. You have now marked the half-pin on the end and the first tail. Mark the second tail slope on the next mark, and the other side of the tail on the last mark. Using the measurements in step 5, you will end up with the tails the same size as the pins.

7 Once the face has been marked, extend the marking over the end grain with a square. From there, use the sliding bevel to repeat the slopes on the reverse. Hatch all the waste areas in pencil and confirm the cuts with a marking knife.

8 Set the wood in the vice so that the slope of one side of the tail is vertical. Using a rip-cut dovetail saw, cut down to just a shade above the line on the waste side of the slope, checking your progress carefully as you go. Take your time and keep checking; the dovetail saw will cut very quickly.

9 Once you have cut all the slopes in one direction, reset the work in the vice so that the opposite slope is vertical and repeat the operation, again taking care not to overcut the line. It is possible to cut these joints with a fine crosscut saw, but it will take a little longer and need more control to prevent the cut from wandering or following the grain.

10 There are several ways of removing the waste from between the tails. It can be sawn out with a fine-bladed fretsaw or coping saw; the bulk of it can be removed by drilling; or, as here, the unwanted material can be chopped away a bit at a time. Take your time and don't try to rush it. Note the piece of softwood being used as a backing board to protect the benchtop. Continue to remove the waste in this manner until you are approaching the line.

11 Use a fine, sharp chisel to remove the final slivers down to the cut line, using a square-edged guide block if you prefer.

12 Remove the sockets for the half-pins at each end with a saw and finish to the line with a sharp chisel. The tails are now cut and ready to be used to mark the position of the pins on the other piece.

13 Mark the length of the pins (which is the thickness of the piece of material with the tails cut into it, plus a whisker for trimming) with a marking gauge.

14 Use the tails you have just cut as a guide to mark the positions of the pins on the end grain. This is best done with a fine knife or a marking awl. A no. 3 scalpel handle fitted with a no. 10a or 11 blade is ideal. The drawer front is secured in the vice and the drawer side laid on top.

15 These scribed lines are then extended down to the gauged line and the waste is hatched with a pencil to reduce the risk of removing the wrong piece.

16 This time the timber is held upright in the vice and you orientate your body to be in line with the cut. Use the dovetail saw to cut down the sides of the pins, a little short of the scribed line, again taking care not to overcut.

17 Remove the waste by chopping out with a chisel, and carefully trim to the line as before.

18 Now your joint should slide together perfectly. If it does not – and mine very rarely do – a bit of light trimming will do the trick. The aim is to get a firm but not a forced fit. There is nothing magic about cutting nice clean dovetails. It is all a matter of experience and practice – lots of practice.

FOCUS ON:
Lapped dovetails

This is the classic drawer-front dovetail. Many a piece of furniture has been sold on the strength of 'those lovely dovetails'. I have to stifle a smile when an eager salesman proudly shows off a set of mass-manufactured machine dovetails as 'a mark of real quality'. Cutting the tails is a similar operation to making through dovetails. The only difference is that the dovetails in this case are shorter than the thickness of the board (typically a drawer front) in which the pins are cut, so that they don't show through the face. I prefer to make the tails $\frac{4}{5}$ (80%) of the thickness of the front. Again, there are no rules; all depends on the size relationship between the two pieces being joined.

Making a lapped dovetail joint

1 The tails are cut as before, and used as a guide to mark the sockets. Using a cutting gauge, scribe the depth of the sockets onto the end grain of the drawer front. Clamp a piece of scrap to the drawer side, in line with the bottom of the tails. Set the drawer front in the vice and place the side on top, using the clamped-on board as a stop so that the end of the side aligns with the gauged line on the drawer front. Mark the slopes using a scalpel or a fine, sharp awl.

2 The depth of the sockets (equal to the thickness of the sides, or very slightly deeper to allow for subsequent trimming) is marked on the rear face of the drawer front with a cutting gauge. The scribed lines for the pins are then squared down to this line, using a marking knife. At this stage it is a good idea to double-check all the marking and, using a soft pencil, hatch all the waste areas.

3 Because the sockets of a lapped dovetail are not cut all the way through, the saw cuts can only go partway. They also have to be made at an uncomfortable angle. Care at this stage will pay off. Set the drawer front high in the vice and, using a dovetail saw, carefully cut at a steep angle on the waste side of the cut line. Do not overcut the gauged lines.

4 Remove the drawer front from the vice and start to chop the waste away with a chisel, working from the end of the board back towards the gauged line. Alternately chop down...

5 ...and then pare out. Take small bites; use gentle but firm taps of the mallet when chopping across the grain, and only hand pressure to trim with the grain. As the chopping progresses, the depth will exceed the saw cut; at this point, light perpendicular cuts with the chisel will be required to deepen the saw cut. These must be done with care in order not to split the grain; light hand pressure is all that is required.

6 Once the full depth has been chopped out, the bottom and sides of the socket can be trimmed using a sharp, narrow paring chisel until the tails can be fitted.

FOCUS ON:
The common dovetail

When joining timber together to make a rectangular frame, this simple joint will add considerable mechanical strength. It is a useful joint to use in an outdoor situation where the timber is going to be exposed to extremes of moisture and temperature.

In this example the joint is being roughly cut into some sawn carcassing to build a frame for a garden store. Although the finish does not need to be as good as one would require for a piece of furniture, the joint must still fit together neatly.

Making a common dovetail

1 Mark the thickness of the pin piece across the face of the tail piece.

2 Set a sliding bevel to at least a 1 : 6 slope, and mark the slope of the tail.

3 Square the marks over the edge and mark the waste.

4 Saw out the waste with a suitable saw; a tenon saw is good for smaller work, but for large construction work a hardpoint saw would be ideal. Trim the tail back to the lines using a large, sharp chisel.

5 Use the tail to mark the socket on the end of the other component, then extend the marks down to the required depth.

6 Remove the material with a saw and chisel, as for a through dovetail...

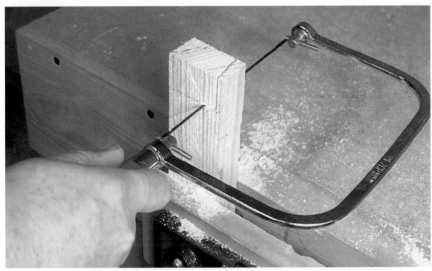

7 ...or remove the waste with a coping saw, as here.

8 Trim and fit the joint.

3:5
Housing (dado) joints

A housing joint (dado in American usage) is used when the entire thickness of a board is to be let into another board. One obvious application is for letting shelves into the sides of bookcases. However, there are many other situations where this joint can be used to good effect. Many pieces of furniture employ a framework in which the horizontal members can be housed into the vertical ones to give mechanical strength in a downwards (or upwards) direction. Drawer dividers in a chest of drawers are another good example of where housings would be the preferred joints to use.

The through housing

The simplest form of housing joint is the through housing. This consists of a trench (housing or dado) cut across the entire width of a board, the width of the trench being the same as the thickness of the board that will be fitted (housed) into it. This joint will be visible from both sides, unless covered with a face frame, veneer or additional finishing trim.

Another popular use for this form of housing is for drawer dividers. Even if the dividers are halved (see Chapter 3:2) where they intersect, the joint between the divider and the drawer box is normally a housing. Making extra housings in the interior of the drawer allows the dividers to be slid in and out to rearrange the storage space within the drawer. There are many other applications for this joint, both in solid timber and in manmade boards.

The secret of cutting any housing joint is crisp, straight shoulders. Accuracy of marking must be the paramount consideration.

Making a through housing

1 Check that the board being inserted into the housing is of a constant thickness along the length of the housing. Any variation will either cause a gap or prevent the board from entering the housing altogether. Mark the position of the housing on the board with a pencil.

2 Check that the line is true by flipping the square over, and, with the stock registering on the same edge as before, recheck the line. When you are satisfied that the line is perfectly square, use a marking knife to confirm the pencil line and sever the grain of the timber, thus ensuring a crisp shoulder the entire length of the housing. Make sure that the knife bevel is facing the waste, ensuring a vertical cut on the showing side.

Key point

If a housing is needed only on one side of the board, a good rule of thumb is for the depth of the housing to be a maximum of half the thickness of the board it is being cut into. If both sides are to be cut, then a maximum of one third the thickness should be employed.

However, different situations may dictate other solutions: for example, if a thin board is being inserted into a much thicker one, then it might be appropriate for the depth of the housing to be quite a small proportion of the thickness of the larger board.

3 Using the width of the board as a gauge, mark the position of the other edge of the housing. Square a line across, referencing from the same edge as you used for the first line. Double-check and confirm with the marking knife.

4 Using a pencil, extend the lines down the edges of the board.

5 Set a gauge to the depth required and scribe a line between the pencil lines on each edge. Confirm the pencil lines down to the gauged lines with a marking knife, and hatch the waste area.

6 A crosscut tenon saw is used to cut carefully down to the gauged line, keeping just inside the knife-cut line. This sounds easier than it is – a long, shallow cut is probably the hardest type of cut to achieve. You can use aids such as blocks of wood to guide the saw (as here), or stops clamped to the blade to govern the depth of cut. However, I invariably find that good, steady, unhurried cutting is the best way in the end.

7 As with all joints, the first time you attempt it will be a learning curve, and practice will improve the technique. So, practise the sawing first on some scrap timber. Mark several parallel lines across the wood and then gauge a depth line. Cut in the parallel lines and extend them down to the gauge line. Now practise cutting; you should see a marked improvement as you progress along the board. Cut on alternate sides of the line in order to simulate the cutting of real housings – it is no use mastering how to cut the left-hand shoulder if the right-hand one gets neglected. The technique of sawing flat is strange at first, and you need to familiarize yourself with the alien stance.

8 Once you have acquired some competence at the sawing, it is time to cut your housing. Saw each shoulder down to the gauged marks, taking care not to overcut them.

9 Using a sharp chisel, remove the bulk of the waste with a paring action. Hand pressure should be adequate. Keep the chisel bevel-down so that there is no risk of cutting too deeply.

10 Once the bulk has been removed, the bottom of the housing can be smoothed with the chisel laid flat, bevel-up, making light, paring slices until the correct depth has been reached. A long paring chisel will cope with longer housings – or a hand router plane can be used for this, if you have one.

11 The board being fitted into the housing should have its end planed flat and square. This can be done either in a vice – with a piece of scrap clamped on to prevent the end breaking out – or on an end-shoot shooting board.

12 Remove the sharp edges with one stroke of a fine-set block plane. This will reduce the risk of any stray fibres turning up as the joint is brought together.

13 Providing all the marking and cutting has been accurate, the other board should slide into the housing with firm pressure applied. If the board is too loose, there is not much that can be done to recover the situation. If it is too tight, then the sides of the housing can be trimmed to accommodate the board. Unless you have a side rebate plane, you will have to use a chisel, and this is not an easy job.

FOCUS ON:
Stopped housings

A housing that stops short of the front edge of the board is used when the face of the piece needs to be finished to a higher standard, or when the part being inserted does not extend to the full width of the board in which the housing is cut.

The problem here is that the saw cannot be swept straight through the joint. There are two schools of thought as to how the stopped cut should be achieved. The 'cut and stop' method (Method 1 below) is the technique I was taught all those years ago, but although it works it is a bit heavy-handed. These days I prefer to use Method 2, where a shallow mortise is cut at the end of the housing before sawing the rest of the shoulders.

Method 1

Mark up as for a through housing, and gauge the length of the housing. Confirm the shoulder lines up to the gauge line. Start cutting with a tenon saw at the open end, slowly lowering the tip until the gauged line is almost reached. Then withdraw the saw and insert the tip into the existing kerf about 25mm (1in) from the gauged stop line. With a sharp, firm movement, applying pressure to the tip, push the blade forward. Withdraw the saw a little further and repeat until the full depth is reached. Repeat for the other shoulder.

The waste is removed as for a through housing, except that as the chisel approaches the stopped end, the end must be chopped down to the level of removal each time, until the full depth is reached.

Method 2

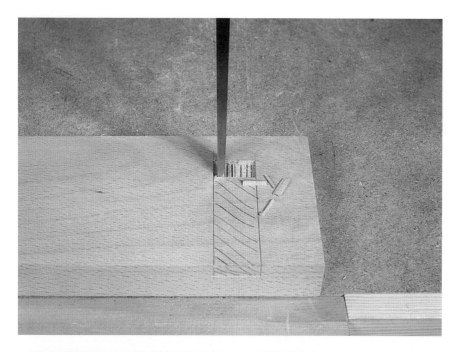

1 Mark up as for Method 1, but this time mark an additional stop line about 25mm (1in) from the final gauged stop mark. Treat this end of the housing as a shallow blind mortise, and chop out the waste accordingly.

2 The shoulders can now be cut through into the mortise, as for a through housing. Remove the waste with a chisel in the normal way.

Notching the housed member

If the board being housed is to extend past the end of the housing, it will need to be notched. This notch must be cut with real care and precision if the joint is to look neat and seamless: too deep and it will leave a gap, too shallow and it will stop the board from seating properly. The aim should be to make the notch *exactly* the same depth as the housing; but, as this is almost impossible with wood, there has to be a minus tolerance. The depth of the notch should be a hair's-width shallower than the housing. This way the cramping will result in a good tight joint between the notch and the face of the first board.

Cutting the notch

Mark the notch with great care and confirm all the lines with a marking knife. Using a fine-toothed saw, cut the notch just inside the knife-cut line and trim to the line with a wide chisel.

FOCUS ON:
Sliding dovetails

This challenging joint is a variation on the standard housing joint, but instead of the shoulders being square they are sloped in towards the top, and the end of the second member – typically a shelf – is cut to match. The advantage of this is that once assembled, the joint can only be disassembled by sliding it apart again – unlike a conventional housing that can be pulled apart. This feature makes it a good choice for tall bookcases, adding mechanical strength to the construction of the carcass. Smaller sliding dovetails can be used in situations where some degree of knock-down is required.

Making a sliding dovetail

1 For the sake of illustration, let us assume that we are fitting a shelf into the carcass of a bookcase. We start by cutting the dovetail socket (housing), and then cut the matching tail into the end of the shelf. Mark up the side of the carcass, making sure that the bottom (widest part) of the dovetail housing is no wider than the thickness of the shelf itself. The ratio of the slope should follow the same rule as for ordinary dovetails (see page 146). Confirm the marked lines with the knife.

2 Saw the sides of the dovetail housing. A guide block will help; this is a piece of timber planed square and true on three sides, with the fourth side planed to the angle of the dovetail. Use this block, clamped to the outside of the cut line, as a fence to guide the saw. It is quite hard to cut at a negative angle and see what you are doing, so if possible try to support the workpiece so that the cut is made vertically. If this is not possible, take care and cut slowly, checking your progress.

3 Remove the waste with a chisel. As long as the saw was held firmly against the guide block, any deviation will have been into the waste area, where it can be cleaned up by trimming with the chisel if necessary.

4 Once the housing has been cut, the shelf is marked to the same depth as the housing and the angle of the tail is marked on each end. The shoulders are sawn, perpendicular to the face, down to the marked slope.

5 The waste is carefully chiselled away. The guide block can be used as before, though packing will be needed to align it. The tail should slide into the housing; do not force it. Careful paring is needed to make the joint fit nicely, and this cannot be hurried. It should be a little looser than most joints – not sloppy, but not tight. Any slight movement in the wood will lock the joint solid, so do not leave it assembled until you are ready to glue up.

The tapered sliding dovetail

The tapered version of the sliding dovetail is self-locking – a friction fit, like a wedge. If anything, this is easier to cut than the ordinary parallel type. The method of marking and cutting is much the same, except for the taper. Fitting is easier, as the joint will not bind until it is almost home, and then a small amount of pressure will drive it in. A swift tap is usually enough to break the joint. When marking the taper, first make sure that the tail is solid enough at the thin end, then expand it from there to a maximum width that is still within the thickness of the timber.

ABOVE *The tapered sliding dovetail is an easier joint to fit together.*

Glossary

Crosscut
Referring to the teeth of a saw, shaped so as to slice through the fibres of the wood while cutting across the grain.

Equilibrium moisture content (EMC)
When the wood is no longer gaining or losing moisture, it has reached an equilibrium with its environment; it has acclimatized to its surroundings.

Face edge
The finished edge of the timber, usually established at 90º to the face side, which is used as a reference when marking.

Face side
The finished face of the timber, used as a reference when marking.

Frog
The bed on which a plane iron is held.

Kerf
The channel created when material is removed by the teeth of a saw.

Long grain
To work long grain is to work with the grain, in the direction of the wood fibres.

Movement
The increase or decrease in the dimensions of wood – more significant across the grain than along it – caused by changes in the immediate environment.

Open time
The length of time an adhesive remains workable in use.

PAR
Planed all round; refers to prepared timber that is supplied with all four faces already planed.

Parallax
The apparent displacement of an object or point caused by a change in the position from which it is viewed.

Rip
To cut along the grain.

Set (of a saw)
The amount by which the teeth are bent out of alignment to provide clearance for the blade when sawing.

Shoot
To plane an edge straight and true.

Index

About the Author

Ralph Laughton originally trained as an engineer, but did not follow that path. Instead, on leaving full-time education he embarked on a career as an editor for a specialist publisher. This led him into the world of graphic design, where he found it possible to indulge a creative passion for well over twenty years.

It was at this point that he decided to take the opportunity to realize a life-long dream. Ralph is now a full-time woodworker, designing and building furniture, repairing old joinery and writing about the techniques that he has spent nearly fifty years acquiring. He is the author of *Success with Sharpening*.

Acknowledgements

Writing a book of this type is a personal thing. Most of what is to be found within these pages is the culmination of years of making sawdust and shavings. The writing of this book was just a case of putting down on paper what I have been applying in practice for years.

Thanks must go to the people who taught me, from my woodwork teachers at school, who introduced me to the basic skills, to my fellow woodworkers of today, from whom I learn something every day.

As usual, my involvement in this book has tested the patience of my good friends in the Magazine Editorial department of GMC.

You can't have a book about joints without wood, so thanks go to South London Hardwoods for allowing me to rummage in their offcuts pile for suitable stock with which to demonstrate the various techniques. Thanks are also due to the good people at Axminster Power Tool Centre, and to Alan Reid of Clico Engineering, the makers of Clifton planes.

Finally I would like to thank my ever-patient wife Sue, who has not only assisted in the writing and photography for this book but has put up with all the sawdust, noise and a grumpy woodworker during the past few months.

Guild of Master Craftsman Publications Ltd,
Castle Place, 166 High Street, Lewes,
East Sussex BN7 1XU, United Kingdom
Tel: +44 (0)1273 488005
www.gmcbooks.com

Contact us for a complete catalogue, or visit our website.